The Nonbeliever's Guide
to the Book of Mormon

The Nonbeliever's Guide to the Book of Mormon

C. B. Brooks, M.D.

PITCHSTONE PUBLISHING
Durham, North Carolina

Pitchstone Publishing
Durham, North Carolina 27705

To contact the publisher, please email info@pitchstonepublishing.com

10 9 8 7 6 5 4 3 2 1

Library of Congress Cataloging-in-Publication Data

Names: Brooks, C. B., author.
Title: The nonbeliever's guide to the Book of Mormon / C.B. Brooks, M.D.
Description: Durham, NC : Pitchstone Publishing, [2017]
Identifiers: LCCN 2016052921| ISBN 9781634311144 (pbk. : alk. paper) | ISBN
  9781634311168 (epdf) | ISBN 9781634311175 (mobi)
Subjects: LCSH: Book of Mormon—Criticism, interpretation, etc.
Classification: LCC BX8627 .B658 2017 | DDC 289.3/22—dc23
LC record available at https://lccn.loc.gov/2016052921

Contents

Section III: Mormonism: An Analysis

Introduction

Maybe you're interested in finding out what Mormons, members of the Church of Jesus Christ of Latter-day Saints, actually believe.

Maybe you've heard that the Mormons believe Jesus Christ visited America.

Maybe you've seen the musical comedy play, *The Book of Mormon*, and wonder if the kooky concepts are real.

Maybe a Mormon missionary has knocked on your door and offered you a book purported to change your life.

But, if you accept the missionary's offer, or contact the church for information, you'll likely be heavily recruited, repeatedly contacted, and pressured to become a member.

Well, here's a no-pressure way to see what's contained in the Book of Mormon, without the hassle of Mormon stalking, and without the tedium and boredom of reading the whole thing. Plus, as an added bonus, this book is written by a nonbeliever, for nonbelievers. No preaching or attempts at conversion here.

After the success of my book *The Nonbeliever's Guide to Bible Stories*, I saw the need for a similar treatment of the Book of Mormon.

Together, we'll fly through each section of the *Book of*

Mormon: An Account Written by the Hand of Mormon upon Plates Taken from the Plates of Nephi with a modern, secular, and often humorous perspective—because there is some wild stuff in there.

Prepare Thyself and Gird Your Loins!

Section I

A BRIEF HISTORY
OF MORMONISM

Unlike many other well-established religions, Mormonism is unique in its recent origins. As a result, its beginnings, evolution, and personalities are well documented, whether through direct eyewitness accounts, government records, and even court cases. This is a good thing, because to truly understand the religion, you need to understand how it arose.

1

Joseph Smith Jr.
and the Golden Plates

Birth of a Prophet

Let's travel back in time to Sharon, Vermont, to the year 1805, where a newborn boy named Joseph Smith Jr. is born into a struggling, not-so-successful farming family. Hoping to improve their situation, they moved to upstate New York, where the Erie Canal project was being planned. The family was somewhat religious and read the Bible. Joseph's grandfather had "religious visions," and a maternal uncle started a small, nonconformist religious community.

Joseph was not a fervently religious boy, but he did attend popular religious revival tent shows that toured the area. These traveling shows featured preachers, miraculous faith healings, speaking in tongues, fainting, convulsions, and, of course, financial collections.

Joseph has been described as somewhat of a slacker, ne'er-do-well, and disorderly person. He took up the occupation of digging in the ground for buried treasure, which was all the rage back then. However, he was lazy and didn't actually like digging. The business plan was to entice local farmers to pay him to look for treasure on their land. It wasn't a blind search, oh no, Joseph would utilize a magic "peep stone," which would allow him to see through the ground, identify where the treasure was buried, and have others do the actual digging. As you can imagine, this endeavor had a very poor success rate and led to Joseph being put on trial for fraud at age twenty-one.

Young Adulthood
Joseph bounced around and met a girl in nearby Pennsylvania and wanted to get married. But her family objected because of Joseph's shady occupation as a money digger, so the couple eloped and had a child around 1827.

Before long, Joseph met and charmed a rich, religiously suggestible neighbor named Martin Harris. Joseph borrowed money from him, and casually shared a fascinating story: Joseph had visions and divine revelations. Martin Harris was intrigued and wanted to know more.

Here's how Joseph told Martin the tale. Seven years earlier, when Joseph was fourteen, he went into the woods alone to pray. It was a nice spring morning, when suddenly a pillar of light brighter than the sun appeared over his head. The light descended slowly until it illuminated him. Two personages were seen hovering above him in midair. One of them spoke to Joseph while pointing at the other person. "This is My Beloved Son. Hear Him!" (Which sounds suspiciously like a Bible verse.)

Whoa. Joseph then asked the floating personages some questions, like, "Which of these religions and traveling tent show preachers should I follow?" And they responded with something like, "None, they're all hackers. We'll let you know sometime in the future."

Yowsa. Martin Harris was hooked by this story! You see, Martin had a past history of seeing religious visions himself and was very superstitious. "Tell me more, Joseph. What happened next?"

A Prophetic Vision

Okay, so Joseph reeled him in with another yarn. One night, about three years after his first divine vision, Joseph—still just a regular farmboy in upstate New York—prayed for another vision before going to bed. Well, sure enough, a heavenly being appeared and identified himself as the angel Moroni, son of another angel named Mormon. Moroni said that God had selected Joseph as the human who will receive some super important information. Moroni gave Joseph directions to go to a nearby hill, named Cumorah, and start digging to find some sacred golden plates that God had hidden there. This was perfect because Joseph was already an experienced treasure digger! These golden plates were engraved in an ancient language and contained updates and the everlasting gospel God wanted everyone to know. The plates had been written originally by Moroni's father, Mormon.

Woo-hoo! Joseph got busy digging and, sure enough, found the plates buried in a stone crate with a round stone lid. Martin Harris couldn't get enough of this story! "What did the plates say? I just gots to know!"

Joseph revealed that Moroni had told him that he couldn't remove the plates without further training, which would take four years! (Sort of like high school, which farmboy Joseph wasn't attending anyway.)

Martin flipped out! "Three years between visions, plus four years of training—and that was seven years ago—why that brings us right up to now! So where are the golden plates? Where? Where?"

Joseph told Martin that he did indeed have the plates in his possession, but Moroni told him to guard them zealously and show them to no one at all. But since Martin was a true believer, Joseph made him a fabulous offer: Martin could become Joseph's partner and help him translate the ancient language engravings on the plates.

Holy cow! Martin jumps all in, starts financially supporting Joseph and his family, and becomes Joseph's personal scribe.

Miraculous Translations

The history of ensuing events has been revised many times. Believers call what happened next a brilliant miracle, while others describe the scenario as a fraud perpetrated on a rich, gullible pawn. Accounts vary. Some say Joseph dictated the contents of the plates to Martin while hiding behind a curtain so Martin couldn't see the alleged plates. Others say that Joseph concealed the plates in an upside down hat and placed two magic seer stones, called the Urim and Thummin, over the opening of the hat. Joseph then reportedly used the stones like goggles to translate the ancient language of the plates hidden inside the hat. Other accounts say Joseph didn't even have the plates while dictating from the hat.

In any case, Joseph would speak the yarn, and Martin would furiously write it down. They collaborated and binge translated 116 pages, which was just the first installment. Martin was so excited that he begged permission to show the pages to others. Joseph had another vision and asked the Lord, but he said no. Martin freaked out again and badgered Joseph. So Joseph asked God again and this time the Lord said, "Well, okay."

Martin ran back to his wife, Lucy, and showed her the pages and told of his wild experience. She said something like, "You've got to be kidding me." But Martin was enthralled and began showing other people! Somehow the pages disappeared. Many think Lucy shredded or burned them.

Martin was devastated and Joseph had a wild hissy fit when he found out. He temporarily lost his prophet's power to translate and banned Martin from scribing, but kept him on the hook for financing.

Joseph prayed hard for guidance and miraculously regained his translation powers, but a "different source" would be used to rewrite the first 116 pages. So they may not be exactly like the missing ones, okay, just in case any discrepancies occur. Joseph recruited a new scribe, Oliver Cowdery, and they spent sixty-five days of uninterrupted feverish work to fully translate the golden plates into the 531-page Book of Mormon.

Good ol' Martin Harris sold off some of his land, mortgaged the rest of his farm, cashed in his savings, and single-handedly paid to have the Book of Mormon: An Account Written by the Hand of Mormon upon Plates Taken from the Plates of Nephi published in 1830 in Rochester, New York.

Lucy filed for divorce.

2

The New Zion (Midwest Edition)

A New Church
Just so people didn't think they were getting scammed, Martin and Oliver and some others swore that they too had a group vision in the woods featuring angel Moroni skimming through the manuscript to inspect the translation and showing them the golden plates. Later in life, Martin admitted he never actually, physically saw the plates, but maintained he saw them in a vision, which is just as good.

Anyway, the lads started up the Church of Christ, based on the Book of Mormon. Later the church's name was updated to the Church of Jesus Christ of Latter-day Saints, commonly called the Mormon Church. Joseph was all of twenty-six years old.

Joseph's idea was for the church to have its own capital city and to make its own laws. A "New Jerusalem or Zion" was planned. Since the United States of the early 1800s was expanding westward, land was available. They recruited followers, called saints, and the business was under way.

The Wild Midwest

The New Zion started off in Kirtland, Ohio, with some shady real estate deals and financing. Joseph was performing "miracles," but received a lot of bad press by failing to restore a dead child back to life. Oliver was having more frequent visions, so Joseph finally sent him off to Missouri to try to convert the Indians. Quarrels broke out amid fraud accusations and unpaid debts. Splinter groups formed.

Joseph was arrested for disorderly conduct twice, and tarred and feathered once by a group led by a radical Mormon apostate. (Wow! How many religions can claim their leader was tarred and feathered? That would make a great painting.) A bank set up by the church failed and accusations of Joseph "enriching himself" abounded.

The neighbors were suspicious of this new secretive religious group of saints with a dodgy bank and started attacking them, eventually driving the Mormons out of Ohio.

Most of the church and saints moved to Missouri where Oliver Cowdrey had been dispatched. Although Joseph liked Ohio better, he too went to join the others in Missouri. The new neighbors in Missouri were even more hostile than the Ohio ones. Fearing the cult's claim that they had a divine right to the land which was to become their own New Zion state, the locals drove the Mormons from Jackson County to Clay County and then to mostly unpopulated Ray County, Missouri.

Unfortunately, Oliver was excommunicated from the church by Joseph, for dishonesty in financial matters and spreading nasty rumors about Joseph. Oliver departed and naturally became a lawyer; he later ran unsuccessfully for political office in Wisconsin.

Back in Missouri, things got better for a while in the more rural surroundings, but that ended in 1838, when the Mormons decided to form both their own military force to defend against outsiders and a secret police force to inform against insiders. They went by names like the Army of Israel, Avenging Angels, and Daughters of Zion.

Riots and small-scale wars broke out between Mormons and non-Mormon Missourians. The Missouri state governor jailed the church leaders and threw the Mormons out! (Sounds like a good time to tar and feather someone again.)

Joseph bribed his way out of jail and moved the Mormons to Illinois and parts of Iowa. Whew! This time, Joseph decided things would be better if he really just took complete control. He bought up land and was promptly accused of enriching himself personally again. He declared the Mormons would set up their own independent government and city called Nauvoo. Joseph formed his own personal army and commissioned himself lieutenant general. The Mormons would be their own self-sufficient entity with Joseph firmly in charge. Woo-hoo Nauvoo.

More Revelations

Around this time, Joseph had numerous revelations directly from God. Rituals and rules were introduced. Good Mormons could advance in the church toward eternal glory and individual godhood. This is where the unusual idea of certain Mormons receiving their own planet after death sprang from.

Joseph also introduced baptisms—not only for the living but also for dead people. He adopted many elements of existing Masonic ceremonies. Secrecy was prized. The growing Mormon rituals included being bathed in water and anointed with oil, wearing special underwear (temple garments), taking oaths and receiving secret names, and pledging to produce many Mormon children.

A Fallen Prophet

Another new program was particularly contentious: polygamy, or plural marriage. Initially, Joseph and the guys in charge started acquiring multiple wives and sex partners from the flock. Some were the very young daughters of fellow Mormons, and others were women already married to other Mormons. When this practice was called into question, Joseph had more religious visions and proclaimed it new official doctrine. A plural marriage "sealing ceremony" was introduced for multiple wives.

This caused much dissension in the ranks, especially among men whose wives and daughters had been poached. One leader, John C. Bennett, major general of the Mormon army, took multiple concubines from the community and didn't even bother marrying them. The church was forced to excommunicate him and he became a vocal critic of Joseph. Counselors of the church started challenging Joseph as a fallen prophet and imposter. More charges of embezzlement and real estate profiteering followed.

Amid internal conflicts and external suspicion, Joseph doubled down on his power grab and decided to launch his political career. He wanted to declare his Mormon experiment an independent state. When he met resistance from the United States government, he played dirty. In 1842, he was charged as an accessory in an attempt to assassinate the governor of Missouri! He fought all attempts of arrest by local sheriffs, by declaring immunity as leader of an independent state. And don't forget he also had his own army!

In 1844, Joseph announced his candidacy for president of the United States. Things were spinning out of control again. Power-mad Joseph ordered the Mormon army to destroy a newspaper printing office that was publishing negative stories about him. His army quickly destroyed the printing office in Carthage, Missouri.

Non-Mormons, the government, and the press had finally had enough. Charges of treason, rioting, and levying war against the state were filed against the Mormons. Joseph and three Mormon leaders were taken into custody and placed in the Carthage jail. That night, a mob of 150 non-Mormons didn't want to wait for trial and stormed the small jail. Joseph was shot in the face, then back, as he jumped from the second-story window trying to escape. The mob descended and finished killing him. Joseph was thirty-nine years old and had led the church for fourteen years.

3

Brigham Young and Utah

An American Moses

Most Mormons viewed Joseph as a martyr and prophet. Some disgruntled saints quit the controversial church. Some Mormons went back east, while others went to Texas and formed a polygamist commune. A group went to Wisconsin and some to Beaver Island in Lake Superior. Another group, including Martin Harris, went back to Kirtland, Ohio.

The Smith family wanted Joseph's son to take over, but Brigham Young, the president of the Governing Council of Twelve, took over the church.

More attacks from anti-Mormons occurred in Nauvoo. Eventually the saints surrendered and agreed to leave immediately. Brigham Young led a group of about ten thousand Mormon believers west on a mass migration by wagon train. They wintered in Nebraska and later continued on to the Great Basin of the Salt Lake in present-day Utah. Brigham Young saw a divine vision that this would be the future Zion. Mormons began building Salt Lake City, which is the headquarters of the current Church of Jesus Christ of Latter-day Saints. Surrounding Mormon communities were established and worldwide outreach missions began shortly thereafter.

The Mormon War

A religious theocratic government ruled during the initial years, known as the provisional state of Deseret. Conflict once again flared, this time with the Mormons violently oppressing non-Mormons who spoke ill of the Prophet Joseph. Even official Mormons were violently coerced to follow strict teachings. "Blood atonement" was an ugly doctrine used by Mormons against nonbelievers and their own who didn't believe strongly enough.

Things got so bad that U.S. President James Buchanan replaced Brigham Young with a non-Mormon governor and sent 2,500 federal troops to keep order. This resulted in the Mormon War. Mormons massacred some civilians. Many left for California. Brigham Young attempted to secede from the United States.

Before long, the war ended when Brigham Young accepted a presidential pardon for his rebellion and agreed to step down as governor. Ol' Martin Harris, the original scribe, joined the Utah group.

The Normalization of Mormonism

Residual Mormon controversies then centered on polygamy, continuation of Mormon religious courts, charges of a shadow government, and discrimination against non-Mormon merchants. Internal squabbles continued with periodic defections from those opposed to Brigham Young, who had 55 wives and 56 children. Lawsuits regarding polygamy made it all the way to the U.S. Supreme Court, which ruled against the Mormon practice in 1879, two years after Young's death.

Congress outlawed the Mormon religious courts. Mormons continued to press for their own religious state, but the tide of history was against them. Once church president Wilford Woodruff put out a statement declaring his intention to submit to U.S. laws against polygamy, the way was cleared for Utah to be admitted to the union. In 1896, Utah became the 45th state.

No longer officially tolerated by the Mormon Church, polygamy went underground and is still practiced in some fundamentalist splinter communities today.

Section II

THE BOOK OF MORMON: AN ACCOUNT WRITTEN BY THE HAND OF MORMON UPON PLATES TAKEN FROM THE PLATES OF NEPHI

TRANSLATED BY JOSEPH SMITH JR.

In this section, I will guide the reader through the text of the Book of Mormon and summarize the various chapters with a contemporary, outsider's view. I'll tell the story in abridged form, hitting the highlights and lowlights, giving the reader a sense of what's in there, without any preaching or attempts at justification. Let's go to the original source and investigate. For your reading pleasure, I'll leave out many of the extraneous characters, places, and items that go nowhere. But don't worry, there are still plenty of twists, turns, and dead ends. And of course, I'll add my own personal commentary, because sometimes I just can't resist!

The Book of Mormon is comprised of some introductory witness statements, then the main text is broken into fifteen sections called Books and named after their alleged narrator, but all are dictated by Joseph Smith Jr. to his faithful scribes.

4

Testimony of Three Witnesses

The Book of Mormon starts off with a short statement by three men: Martin Harris, Oliver Cowdery, and David Whitmer. They swear that they have seen not only the golden plates but also the engravings on the plates that record the history of the people of Nephi, Jared, and the Lamanites.

They further declare, with words of soberness—so no one can accuse them of being drunk—that they also saw an angel of God come down from heaven, who showed them the plates and engravings. Furthermore, they heard the voice of God command them, in no uncertain terms, that they should bear witness to this as true.

Note: as already mentioned, Martin later said when questioned that he only saw the plates in a vision, not in real life. Oliver was driven from the church for financial fraud. And David was a friend of Oliver's, who also only saw the plates in a vision. Whitmer lived with the Mormons in Ohio but fled to Missouri to avoid arrest after the bankruptcy of the Mormon bank. He later condemned Joseph and left the church.

5

Testimony of Eight Witnesses

Okay, so the three witnesses were a little weak, but behold, here come eight more: four Whitmers, three Smiths, and one Hiram Page. They offer a shorter statement, again with soberness, in which they declare that Joseph Smith Jr. actually showed them the plates and that they handled them with their own hands. They swear that Joseph has the plates. And they lie not.

Some sources say Joseph allowed others to handle the alleged plates, but they were covered in cloth and not able to be seen.

Note: to date, no other human has claimed to have seen any of these sacred plates. After the Book of Mormon was published in 1830, Joseph Smith said he returned the plates to the angel Moroni, so that explains why. Hiram Page would continue in the church, until he was excommunicated along with Whitmer in 1833.

6

First Book of Nephi

Okay, sports fans, finally we get to the actual tale told by Joseph Smith to his scribes and followers. This book is divided into twenty-two chapters and reportedly comes from the small plates of Nephi. (Because remember, the first translation written down by Martin Harris was "inadvertently" left in a shredder, or fireplace, meaning the earlier history is retold in a slightly different way in this book. So any inconsistencies that people might recall are due to this second set of plates, not Joseph's less-than-photographic memory. Glad we got that straight.)

Our story begins around year 600 BC in the Middle East, somewhere near Jerusalem. Zedekiah is the current King of Judah. Many prophets are cruising around warning people to repent, or else Jerusalem will be destroyed.

Nephi, son of Lehi, is the narrator of this book. He declares that it is true and made by his own hand. Nephi tells of his father, Lehi, being confronted by a pillar of fire above a rock. Then Lehi was elevated to heaven, where he saw singing angels and God himself sitting on a throne brighter than the sun. Twelve others gave Lehi a book listing all the abominations going on in Jerusalem and warning of destruction and capture by nearby Babylon.

Lehi starts a career as a prophet. His son, Nephi, writes down with his own hands an abridged version of his dad's visions and prophecies upon special plates. The local Jews didn't appreciate Lehi telling them how wicked they were and how badly they were behaving, and repeatedly threatened his life. Lehi forged ahead anyway, predicting a future Messiah too.

God supported Lehi with numerous dreams and advice. God commanded him to take his family out into the wilderness. Lehi agreed and left his house, gold, silver, and possessions behind, and dragged his family down to the remote border of the Red Sea where they camped in tents. The group consisted of Lehi, his wife, and four sons: Laman, Lemuel, Sam, and Nephi. Dad gave lots of speeches and proclamations. Nephi enjoyed hearing them; Laman and Lemuel certainly did not. So God also started talking to Nephi, promising to make him a great teacher, and also promising to curse his rebellious brothers.

God tells Nephi that a big shot back in Jerusalem named Laban has an accurate history of the Jews and a genealogy of Lehi's family engraved on brass plates, and Nephi and his brothers should go back to the big city, get them, and bring the plates back to the wilderness. The brothers pack some tents and head to Jerusalem. They arrive at the house of Laban and cast lots to see who will do the talking. Laman loses and has to go in to ask Laban to give up the plates. Well, Laban listens and is supremely ticked off and threatens to kill Laman, but instead he just throws him out.

The brothers hatch a plan. They go back to their old house and pick up all the gold, silver, and cash that their dad, Lehi, left behind. They bring it all to Laban and offer to buy the brass record plates. Laban has a better idea; he sends his servants to grab the treasure and kill the brothers instead. Behold, the boys drop the loot and run away. They hightail it back to the wilderness and hide.

The plan is a complete failure. After they catch their breath, Laman and Lemuel speak some rather harsh words to their younger brothers and even spank Nephi with a rod. While the ass whuppin' is going on, an angel of the Lord appears and basically says, "Why do you smite your young bro? God has chosen him to be a boss man over you. Now get back to Jerusalem and get those plates Goddammit."

Nephi gives them a pep talk and they sneak back toward Laban's house at night. Nephi comes upon a passed-out drunk dude lying on the sidewalk. Lo and behold, it is the big shot Laban himself. Nephi removes Laban's fancy sword from its scabbard and has a back-and-forth debate with the Spirit of God about killing Laban. Finally, Nephi sees that God is right: it's totally cool to kill an unfaithful man in an attempt to get the population to listen to God's commandments and the Law of Moses. Makes sense, I guess. So Nephi obeys the Spirit, grabs Laban by the hair, and lops his head off with his own fancy sword. Ouch.

Nephi then dresses up in Laban's rich garments and armor and walks into his house. He meets the servant who has the keys to Laban's treasury vault. Nephi miraculously speaks in the voice of Laban and says, "Open it up." Nephi and the servant grab the gold, silver, plates, and jewelry, then go outside where the brothers are waiting. The servant, Zoram, figures things out but swears an oath to become a loyal follower of the boys.

Upon return to the family campground in the wilderness, dad Lehi is thrilled, especially because he was taking heat from mom who thought the boys had probably died. Now she's a believer and won't complain about everyone having visions and not cleaning up. Time for some sacrifices and burnt offerings to the awesome God of Israel.

Forthwith, Lehi gets busy and starts reading the special brass plates. They contain the first five books of the Bible, also known as the Law of Moses, featuring Creation with Adam and Eve, and later Exodus from Egypt. Bible prophets are quoted, including Jeremiah. A history of the Jews right up to the current King Zedekiah is recorded, including family trees showing that Lehi was a direct descendant of Joseph and Jacob of biblical fame.

Lehi was loving this and prophesied that these brass plates will endure and be carried by his offspring seed into the future.

Family Drama

Lehi finally calms down enough to receive another message from God, who thinks it's time for Lehi's sons to take wives and procreate, and who wants Lehi to send his sons up to Jerusalem again to bring his old friend Ishmael out into the wilderness.

Okay, so Nephi and his brothers tarry in the city to convince Lehi's friend, Ishmael, to drag himself and his family to the wilderness camp.

On the way, drama ensues. Laman and Lemuel, along with two of Ishmael's cranky daughters and two uprooted sons, start "murmuring," complaining, and finally rebel not only against Nephi and his young brother Sam but also against Ishmael, his wife, and three well-behaved daughters. The rebels want to go back to Jerusalem, probably to party and get wicked.

This gives Nephi a perfect opportunity to remind them about his divine visions, the appearance of angels, God's help in slaying Laban, and how everyone in Jerusalem is going to perish when God gets mad enough—which is going to be soon. The rebels aren't convinced and tie Nephi up with cords, then scheme to ditch him in the woods to be eaten by wild beasts.

Nephi prays to God and the cords come loose. Nephi spake unto the rebels again and this second time his words work— they all become sorrowful and repent. The posse regroups, continues onward to the tent of Lehi, and enjoy some more burnt offerings.

Later, Lehi describes a big vision about good people who follow God's rules, people like his wife Sariah, sons Nephi and Sam, and those who accept God's teachings. He sees them as eating the sweet fruit of a special tree, at the end of a straight and narrow path, near a lovely river. There are also multitudes of people who don't partake of the fruit, including hordes who cram into a big floating cathedral in the sky and mock those who are partaking of the wonderful fruit. The worst news of all is that his own misbehaving sons, Laman and Lemuel, don't accept the fruit. When he returns to reality, Lehi exhorts the sons to follow God's commandments, then completely stops speaking to them.

Shifting Gears

Nephi, our narrator (who's really Joseph Smith), then explains that there are actually two sets of plates. The first set will form the rest of this current book and focus on the religious ministry of his people. The second set, also called the plates of Nephi, will tell the history of wars and kings. That's the way of the Lord commanded him to do it, okay.

Nephi spends the next chapters of this first book of Nephi telling of the visions he's seen concerning the religious future of Palestine. It's predominantly a big rehash of the Christian Bible and includes the following: Jerusalem is sacked, and Jews become captives of the Babylonians and will return out of captivity and repossess their promised land. Six hundred years after Lehi passes, a messiah, the son of God, is born via a virgin birth in Nazareth. Someone else (not mentioned by name) will prepare the Messiah's way by baptizing people and the young savior too. The Jews will kill the son of God, who will then rise from the dead and, by the power of the Holy Ghost, reveal himself to the Gentiles.

Nephi also sees the Tree of Life, Lamb of God, crucifixion, and twelve apostles. Curiously, the names Jesus, Mary, John the Baptist, and individual apostles are not yet mentioned, even though direct quotes are lifted from the Bible. Nephi also describes the Great Judgment at the end of the world, with the Lamb of God Messiah descending again to earth. A huge battle between Nephi's descendants will be fought against the devil and descendants of his lousy brothers. The seed of Nephi will lose the battle and the winners will fall into disbelief, filth, and idleness.

That's not all—the devil then starts his own abominable

church, made up of Gentiles, on Earth. This evil church kills saints, collects gold, riches, and even employs harlots!

The devil's church becomes very successful, mostly by leaving out important parts of God's gospel. But the Lamb of God will win again in the future because of the information on the brass plates. A new Zion will form, composed of white, fair, beautiful people who follow a book derived from the plates. (Hmmm, sounds just like the fledgling Mormon Latter-day Saints Church Joseph Smith is starting!) This is the only way to be saved. Woe unto any Gentile or Jew who doesn't join up. You're either with us or against us. There are only two choices: our new church, or the abominable church of the devil that encompasses everyone else. Hell and the "whore of the earth" await all except the few saints of God who are true believers.

War and the wrath of God loom ahead. The narrator throws in lots of terms borrowed from the Bible's Book of Revelation. Nephi even has a vision of John (who was the author of Revelation) attesting that all these things are true. More foreshadowing: Nephi senses there's more to come, much more, but he won't tell us yet.

Back to the Tent
After the preceding lengthy apocalyptic rant, mercifully for the reader, Nephi returns to Lehi's tent in the wilderness, where his brothers are arguing. They can't understand the prophecies, so Nephi tries to explain the previous flights of oratory.

The brothers are bummed out, because it sounds like they're destined to be cast into hell. But Nephi cheers them up by saying something to the order of, "Dumbasses, clean up your acts and maybe you'll be saved."

Nephi, Laman, Lemuel, and Sam all marry daughters of Ishmael. Even Zoram, the servant, gets to marry the oldest daughter (because older girls are less desirable).

And it came to pass that God commanded Lehi to move the extended family further along the coast of the Red Sea. God pointed the way with a special spindle fixed on a fine brass ball.

Food is scarce and Nephi accidentally breaks his bow and arrow. Laman, Lemuel, and Ishmael's sons start murmuring obscenities again, even complaining about the Lord!

Lehi asks God where they can get food, and God is not amused about the murmuring. He tells Lehi to read the goddamn directions inscribed on the ball. Oh, who knew there were directions scrawled there? Sure enough, they point Nephi to a mountaintop where he can slay some dinner for the group.

Ishmael dies and his daughters start bitching about leaving Jerusalem in the first place. They're sick of this wilderness sojourning. Laman and Lemuel agree with them and consider murdering dad Lehi and brother Nephi. God intervenes and talks them out of it, over a nice dinner.

Let's Build a Boat
The gang roams around the wilderness along the Red Sea for eight more years. During that time the wives bear children. God provides things to eat from the land and they call the area Bountiful.

God speaketh to Nephi and tells him to start building a ship. The boat will take them to the promised land. God instructs him how to find or manufacture tools. His older brothers start to murmur against him, then openly start complaining about the ship-building project. Then they threaten to throw him into the sea.

Nephi goes off on a long rant recounting all the great things Moses did for forty years while leading the Jews out of Egypt. He tells them he's following the same path by leading the family out of Jerusalem, which need I remind you, is going to be destroyed pretty soon for wickedness.

God backs Nephi up by warning that if the brothers even so much as touch Nephi, they'll shrivel up like dried reeds. The brothers are spooked and start helping Nephi build the boat.

The boat gets finished around 590 BC and God tells everyone to get on board, including old dad Lehi, who apparently got lucky and begat two more sons whilst in the wilderness, named Jacob and Joseph. The group shoves off for the promised land.

They had smooth sailing for many days, navigating with a new invention, the compass, that God made especially for them. Things go well on the high seas until Laman, Lemuel, their wives, and the sons of Ishmael start a nautical happy hour. They sing, dance, and use bad language! Captain Nephi admonishes them because he knows the Lord would not approve. The party people get fed up with young brother Nephi always being a wet blanket, so Laman and Lemuel tie him up with cords again.

When God hears of this, he sends a violent tempest and stops the compass from working! The storm lasts four days and the partiers become seasick, miserable, and lost on the turbulent oceans. Finally they untie Nephi and repent. So God calms the seas and fixes the compass malfunction. Nephi successfully sails the ship to the land of promise.

The ship eventually runs aground on a new continent. It truly is a promised land, with good dirt for farming, forests, cows, goats, asses, horses, and plenty of gold, silver, and copper.

The Book of Mormon does not officially say whether this new promised land is the Americas, but the Mormon Church concludes that it is. And it makes sense if you believe that Joseph Smith actually found the plates in his upstate New York backyard. But throughout the entire Book of Mormon, the word America never appears. Additionally, the names of the many places and territories in the promised land that appear in the book are geographically vague. There's no map and there are no clear reference points; it's just assumed we know these locations.

Let's Make Some Plates

The Lord commanded Nephi to start making some brass plates and then to engrave upon them the history of his forefathers and the many events yet to come. Prophets named Zenos and Zenock predict that in about six hundred years God the Redeemer will show up in Jerusalem, and the Jews will scourge and crucify him, but he'll rise after three days of darkness.

As punishment for this crucifixion crime, the Jews shall wander the earth and perish, plus be hated by everybody in the meantime. Descendants of Nephi's group (who are currently Jews) and any Gentiles who repent and follow the covenants will be exempted and saved.

A few chapters of wild, babbling religious oratory follow. Here's a taste:

1 Nephi 21

1 And again: Hearken, O ye house of Israel, all ye that are broken off and are driven out because of the wickedness of the pastors of my people; yea, all ye that are broken off, that are scattered abroad, who are of my people, O house of Israel. Listen, O isles, unto me, and hearken ye people from far; the Lord hath called me from the womb; from the bowels of my mother hath he made mention of my name.

2 And he hath made my mouth like a sharp sword; in the shadow of his hand hath he hid me, and made me a polished shaft; in his quiver hath he hid me;

3 And said unto me: Thou art my servant, O Israel, in whom I will be glorified.

1 Nephi 21

7 Thus saith the Lord, the Redeemer of Israel, his Holy One, to him whom man despiseth, to him whom the nation abhorreth, to servant of rulers: Kings shall see and arise, princes also shall worship, because of the Lord that is faithful.

1 Nephi 21

8 Thus saith the Lord: In an acceptable time have I heard thee, O isles of the sea, and in a day of salvation have I helped thee; and I will preserve thee, and give thee my servant for a covenant of the people, to establish the earth, to cause to inherit the desolate heritages;

1 Nephi 21

12 And then, O house of Israel, behold, these shall come from far; and lo, these from the north and from the west; and these from the land of Sinim.

1 Nephi 21

13 Sing, O heavens; and be joyful, O earth; for the feet of those who are in the east shall be established; and break forth into singing, O mountains; for they shall be smitten no more; for the Lord hath comforted his people, and will have mercy upon his afflicted.

A final chapter is presented explaining that this was all the Voice of the Spirit, so here's what all that bluster actually meant. The house of Israel will sooner or later be scattered across the planet. The Lord will then create a mighty nation from the Gentiles. Wars between religions and against the devil's church will occur. Anyone who fights against Zion will be destroyed. It's written on the plates of brass and all certified again as true.

7

Second Book of Nephi

This book contains thirty-three chapters. The first four are Lehi's farewell speeches.

The group is now in the promised land and father Lehi is getting old. So he begins to speak, and speak, and speak. The first chapter is Lehi speaking to Nephi's no-good older brothers, Laman and Lemuel. He recounts all the bad things they've done, and how great and merciful God is for not drowning them, or worse. Lehi also mentions how God has covenanted this new promised land to Lehi and his children forever. That's a long-term legal deed. But there's a condition— everyone must follow God's commandments, or else they'll be cut off from God's presence and destroyed. Okay, sons, now put on some armor of righteousness, listen to Nephi, and fly right.

Lehi's two newest sons, Jacob and Joseph, each get their own chapters with dedicated farewell speeches from Lehi. They contain a big rehash of Bible references, things we heard already in Nephi 1, like a messiah will redeem mankind and the devil is the father of all lies. Some don't make much sense: Adam and Eve sinned so man could know joy?

More speeches to Sam, Zoram, and the kids of the brothers. More talk of human seeds, fruits of loins, warnings—and finally Lehi dies and is buried.

A few days later, Laman and Lemuel start getting angry with their younger brother Nephi, mostly because he's always quoting scripture and rules and delivering holier than thou speeches; which can get annoying.

By the fifth chapter, we finally get back to our story. Understandably, the older brothers decide to slay Nephi so they won't have to listen to him anymore. God tells Nephi to gather anyone loyal and flee into the wilderness, which he does. The loyal group consists of Nephi's family, brother Sam and his family, Zoram the former servant of Laban and his crew, and Lehi's recent offspring Jacob and Joseph.

As the story goes, they journeyed into the wilderness, pitched tents, and called themselves the "people of Nephi, or Nephites." Oh, and they followed all God's statutes and commandments and laws. Their crops and animal herds thrived because the Lord was with them. Prosperity reigned in exile. They also brought the brass plates, direction ball, and compass from the boat. Nephi also smuggled out the sword of that old Jerusalemite bully Laban and figured out how to mass-produce copies of it. The people of Nephi built a temple, metal and wooden buildings, and mine abundant gold, silver, and copper. Nephi was appointed King.

Things were not going well at all for Nephi's difficult older brothers, Laman and Lemuel. The Lord had cut them off from his presence and that usually makes for bad times. The problem brothers and their descendants were called Lamanites, and they now hated the prosperous Nephites.

2 Nephi 5

14 And I, Nephi, did take the sword of Laban, and after the manner of it did make many swords, lest by any means the people who were now called Lamanites should come upon us and destroy us; for I knew their hatred towards me and my children and those who were called my people.

2 Nephi 5

20 Wherefore, the word of the Lord was fulfilled which he spake unto me, saying that: Inasmuch as they will not hearken unto thy words they shall be cut off from the presence of the Lord. And behold, they were cut off from his presence.

In one of the most politically incorrect moves God ever made, he turned the skin of the previously white, good-looking Lamanites the color of black—so they would be loathsome and easily recognizable, completely unattractive, and unable to integrate with the fair-skinned Nephites. The Lord charred them like a flint fire! And God cursed their seed should it ever mix with the white Nephites.

2 Nephi 5

21 And he had caused the cursing to come upon them, yea, even a sore cursing, because of their iniquity. For behold, they had hardened their hearts against him, that they had become like unto a flint; wherefore, as they were white, and exceedingly fair and delightsome, that they might not be enticing unto my people the Lord God did cause a skin of blackness to come upon them.

22 And thus saith the Lord God: I will cause that they shall be loathsome unto thy people, save they shall repent of their iniquities.

23 And cursed shall be the seed of him that mixeth with their seed; for they shall be cursed even with the same cursing. And the Lord spake it, and it was done.

These passages contributed greatly to charges that the Mormon Church harbored a deep-rooted racism against black people. For example, the Church had a long-standing policy preventing black people from becoming Mormon priests, although they could be church members. Pressure against the Church mounted until 1978, when the Church president had a divine revelation in which God decided to allow blacks into the Mormon priesthood.

Back to our story. God further cursed the Lamanites and they became an Idle people, sneaky, scourges, and full of mischief.

The Nephites, on the other hand, were doing great. Nephi promoted Jacob and Joseph to become priests. Everyone was happy. God told Nephi to make more metal plates and engrave all of their conversations.

Forty years go by. Some wars against the Lamanites are briefly mentioned. Jacob starts preaching and rambles on the same topics and prophecies as Lehi and Nephi did. Sounds very much like the doom and gloom prophets of the Old

Testament. He adds a bunch of woes: woe unto the rich, blind, deaf, whores, liars, idol worshipers, etc. Same message: better repent, you people.

An angel tells Jacob that the Messiah's name will be Christ, and he will come among the Jews, who are the most wicked nation, and they'll crucify him. Jews will pay for this with famines, pestilence, and death—and any survivors will be scattered across the earth. But, if they repent and believe, they can be saved.

Jacob and Nephi combine to produce chapters of incoherent blathering with references to the Bible's Isaiah. Some nuggets: the Lord says to call the prophetess's new son Maher-shalal-hash-baz, reveals a virgin shall conceive, hisses for the bee in Assyria, and conveys important information on oxen and lesser cattle.

2 Nephi 16

1 In the year that king Uzziah died, I saw also the Lord sitting upon a throne, high and lifted up, and his train filled the temple.

2 Above it stood the seraphim; each one had six wings; with twain he covered his face, and with twain he covered his feet, and with twain he did fly.

3 And one cried unto another, and said: Holy, holy, holy, is the Lord of Hosts; the whole earth is full of his glory.

4 And the posts of the door moved at the voice of him that cried, and the house was filled with smoke.

2 Nephi 18

1 Moreover, the word of the Lord said unto me: Take thee a great roll, and write in it with a man's pen, concerning Maher-shalal-hash-baz.

2 And I took unto me faithful witnesses to record, Uriah the priest, and Zechariah the son of Jeberechiah.

3 And I went unto the prophetess; and she conceived and bare a son. Then said the Lord to me: Call his name, Maher-shalal-hash-baz.

2 Nephi 19

20 And he shall snatch on the right hand and be hungry; and he shall eat on the left hand and they shall not be satisfied; they shall eat every man the flesh of his own arm—

21 Manasseh, Ephraim; and Ephraim, Manasseh; they together shall be against Judah. For all this his anger is not turned away, but his hand is stretched out still.

Eventually Nephi gets back on topic and tells everyone that after Christ is crucified and rises from the dead three days later, he's going to come and visit the Nephites in their new continent! Christ will give more law and teachings, and also wreak vengeance on anyone who is wicked or has killed prophets and saints.

However, four generations after Christ appears to the people of Nephi, a speedy destruction will cometh unto them! They'll embrace the devil and be sentenced to hell. Nephi's definitely depressed at the prophecy, but he knows God's ways are just. Yup, when you dwindle into unbelief, you'll be smitten by the Gentiles. Makes sense.

A Prophecy of the Future Book of Mormon and Joseph Smith

The Gentiles will eventually take over the land of the Nephites and some Jews will be scattered around. Iniquity and bad behavior will abound. It will be like a deep sleep has fallen over mankind and no one will know how to live.

But don't despair. God shall reveal, to a chosen man (presumably Joseph Smith), the special information that will be written up in a sealed book (presumably the Book of Mormon). Three witnesses will attest to it (sounds familiar).

When the Lord is ready, the book shall be revealed describing the foundation of the world and its final fiery judgment. When the book is revealed, it will be shouted from the rooftops. The source of the book (the plates) shall only be seen by a few witnesses, then God will command the chosen person to seal up the plates again and send them back to God. When God's ready, he'll reveal everything, since some of the information is still secret. Woe to those who don't believe and any who fight against Zion.

This is a pretty self-serving prophecy. Joseph Smith is actually the one speaking it out of a hat to his scribe, although he's using the character of Nephi as narrator of this section—but it's still Joseph Smith talking. Although he doesn't mention himself or the title of the book by name, the implication is highly transparent.

Before getting back to more prophecies about the end of the world, he throws in another plug for the Book of Mormon:

it will be of tremendous worth to our descendants. Okay, got it. Lots of false churches will exist, and they're all wrong and corrupt, and did I also mention that that abominable whore-of-the-earth—the church of the devil—will also be around too? Woe be unto everybody because all those who don't repent will be destroyed—I'm sure I did mention that a couple hundred times already.

For any doubters who might be wondering why we even need another holy book since we already have the Bible, we get our answer here. God reveals that yes, he's god of the whole world and all the nations and that he already spake to the Jews in the Middle East, and to the Nephites, and also to other tribes—and he told them all to write down his words at different times—but you're super-duper lucky, because you're getting access to this most important new book.

In the final chapters, Nephi gives a long, repetitious farewell speech of flowery oratory reminding everyone, Gentile or Jew, that if they repent, follow God's rules, get baptized with water, stay on the straight path and go through the narrow gate, accept the Father, Son, and Holy Ghost, repent some more, speak with the tongues of angels, and do everything as directed: you can have eternal life. Finally, Nephi bids adieu and stops preaching.

8

Book of Jacob

Jacob, remember him? One of the sons Lehi sired late in life, and the much younger brother of Nephi. Now it's Jacob's turn to narrate a book.

Rejoice all ye readers! Jacob's book is much shorter—only seven chapters—hallelujah! After slogging through the interminable Nephi 1 and 2, this is much appreciated. Maybe Jacob hired an editor?

Fifty-five years have passed since the group set sail from Jerusalem to the New World, putting us now around 545 BC. Nephi is now very old and commands Jacob to pass down Nephi's plates to each generation. Also, Jacob should start a new set of small plates and engrave on them any divine revelations, preaching, or other noteworthy news. Jacob agrees.

The people loved Nephi, who protected them with the sword of Laban, and Nephi dies. In his honor, they decide to call their future rulers: Second Nephi, Third Nephi, etc.

Jacob points out that the descendants of the other original members of the sailing party were known as Lamanites,

Lemuelites, and Ishmaelites, but for simplicity purposes, all those unfriendly to the Nephites would now be called Lamanites. Thank you for that.

Okay, back to live action. Under the reign of the Second Nephi King, the Nephites started to get unruly and indulge in wicked pastimes, like taking concubines and hoarding gold. Jacob and his brother Joseph, having been designated priests, speak out against this. The grossest crime of all is taking more than one wife and any amount of concubines. It is an abominable whoredom! (How the later Mormons justified polygamy with this passage is incredible!) Jacob even says it's a worse iniquity than those stinking, dark-skinned Lamanites. So cut out the fornicating and avoid destruction from God already.

Jacob 2

27 Wherefore, my brethren, hear me, and hearken to the word of the Lord: For there shall not any man among you have save it be one wife; and concubines he shall have none;

28 For I, the Lord God, delight in the chastity of women. And whoredoms are an abomination before me; thus saith the Lord of Hosts.

35 Behold, ye have done greater iniquities than the Lamanites, our brethren. Ye have broken the hearts of your tender wives, and lost the confidence of your children, because of your bad examples before them; and the sobbings of their hearts ascend up to God against you. And because of the strictness of the word of God, which cometh down against you, many hearts died, pierced with deep wounds.

Jacob launches into some long-winded speeches about repentance, olive trees, and salvation only being through belief in Jesus Christ (who isn't even born yet, but is now mentioned by name).

In the last chapter, an interesting character named Sherem shows up. Sherem is a Nephite, who was a pretty good debater and challenges Jacob's teachings. He and Jacob debate head-to-head, one-on-one, with Sherem arguing there will be no Christ coming in a few hundred years. Then he calls Jacob a blasphemer and asks for a sign showing Jacob is right. Well, this was not a good tactical move. Jacob calls up the Spirit of God, and Sherem falls to the dirt floor. He's down but not dead. Sherem whispers, begging the audience to come back tomorrow, when he's feeling better. The next day he tells everyone that he had been deceived by the devil and dies right there. How's that for a sign, smartass Sherem?

Jacob struggles in vain to convince the Lamanites to repent but gets nowhere. The filthy Lamanites just hate the Nephites and attack them regularly in military battles (none are described though). The people of Nephi defend themselves.

Jacob goes to his grave but passes the plates on to his son, Enos.

9

Book of Enos

Enos, my man, one brief chapter—you rock! Your uncle Nephi could have learned something from you.

Enos was hunting in the woods and decided to pray for forgiveness. The voice of God answered and absolved his sins, then started to chat. Enos asked God to help out the Nephites and also to please try again to save the Lamanites. His reasoning went like this: just in case the Nephites get destroyed, but the Lamanites survive, then God could preserve the sets of plates recording the history of the Nephites and reveal the plates to the surviving Lamanites sometime in the future. God says okay because he knows Enos is sincere.

More battles are alluded to between the Nephites and Lamanites. All efforts to convert the Lamanites fail. Descriptions of the Lamanites mirror the popular depictions of Native Americans in the nineteenth-century imagination. They have dark skin, are wild, ferocious, and bloodthirsty, eat raw meat, live in teepees, wear loincloths, and use hatchets and bow and arrows. They also despise the white Nephites, who desire only to farm the land, live in peace, and raise nice animals like cattle, goats, and horses.

Enos witnesses many wars between the Lamanites and Nephites, then grows old and dies. It's now 179 years since Lehi and the group left Jerusalem for the promised land, putting the date around 421 BC.

10

Book of Jarom

A new narrator, Jarom, son of Enos, appears. Lucky for us, he's inherited Enos's gift of brevity.

Jarom has a few things to add to the small plates, but he says he'll skip the prophesying and lengthy transcription of his divine communications, because what more could he say that hasn't already been beaten into us. (Author's note: I think I found a favorite character.)

Most of the people still have hardened hearts, blind eyes, and stiff necks, and are quite lucky God hasn't killed them yet. Even so, many of the Nephites are still good and follow the rules. Lamanites are still hopeless, however, attacking the Nephites and drinking the blood of wild beasts—their usual bad behavior.

Both groups multiplied and spread out across the land. The Nephites held their own, fortifying their cities against Lamanite incursions. Nephite prophets continually reminded their people to keep the commandments, and things were relatively good.

Jarom hands the plates off to his son, Omni, around 399 BC.

11

Book of Omni

A fast relay race through about two hundred years of history, with the baton handed off to different narrators.

Omni writes some notes onto the plates. He says he's not really a good person and he killed many Lamanites with his sword while defending his people of Nephi. The defenses worked and they had many years of peace. He hands off the plates to his son, Amaron.

Amaron reports that the Lord got fed up with the portion of the Nephite population that didn't follow the commandments and smote them. The righteous Nephites were preserved. Plates get delivered to his brother, Chemish.

Chemish says that Amaron pretty much covered it and passes them to his son, Abinadom.

Abinadom reports many wars with Lamanites and says he personally killed many by his sword. His son, Amaleki, takes the plates.

Amaleki has some news. God warns the current King of Nephites, Mosiah, that they should flee the land of the Nephites and go into the wilderness. Mosiah leads the faithful on a long trek with God's help and directions. Prophets continually badgered everyone about the usual things—repentance and rules.

The group discovered a new tribe of inhabitants in the land of Zarahemla. The new tribe welcomed Mosiah and the Nephites when they showed them the plates of brass containing the record of the Jews.

Why? Because it turns out the people of Zarahemla also fled from Jerusalem around the time that King Zedekiah of Judah was captured by the Babylonians!

The Zarahemlas wandered around the wilderness of the Middle East for a while until God led them across the ocean to the promised land too. No mention of how, but they got there. They suffered through some wars but multiplied quite well. Unfortunately, their language had been corrupted and they brought no written records, so the Nephites couldn't understand them.

No bother, Mosiah taught them the Nephite language, and the two tribes united as Nephites under King Mosiah. The oral genealogy of the Zarahemlas was remembered and engraved on a brand new set of plates.

A weird story is mentioned about a large stone with engravings being brought to King Mosiah. He translates it, using the power of God, and learns of a man named Coriantumr and his slain people, who the Zarahemlas discovered in the New World. Coriantumr's parents also came out from the Middle East during the time of the Tower of Babel. No further details are given, at least for now.

Anyway, King Mosiah dies and his son, Benjamin, takes

over as ruler. The Lamanites show up and fight against the newly merged Nephites, who knock the Lamanites out of the land of Zarahemla.

Amaleki has no sons, so he gives the plates to King Benjamin.

But before Amaleki goes, a final tale is told of some Nephites moving out to reclaim their original promised land. Their leader was stiffnecked and caused contention. All were slain except fifty, who returned. Another larger group also embarks for the wilderness, including Amaleki's brother, who he never sees again.

With that, Amaleki leaves us hanging. It's around 130 BC.

12

The Words of Mormon

Not listed as a book, just as some words from Mormon. A different Book of Mormon chapter appears later in the overall Book of Mormon volume.

This is weird—strap into your time machine and fast-forward. A person named Mormon speaks to us from centuries later. He declares that it's now many hundreds of years after Christ's arrival on planet Earth. Mormon is preparing the plates to give to his son, Moroni. He's witnessed the near-total destruction of his Nephite people.

Mormon explains that he's condensed or abridged the plates of Nephi from their beginning, all the way to Amaleki's engravings in the time of King Benjamin, which we just heard about. He's also included in his record the new set of small plates from the time of Jacob to King Benjamin.

Mormon is pleased, because the prophecies about Christ coming to earth, around zero BC or one AD, have all actually happened. So that's a good sign that future prophecies will also come true.

I'm not sure, but it seems like there are an awful lot of plates floating around. Maybe Joseph Smith's lost track of what's been dictated to his scribe? Or maybe the scribe is questioning, like me, and trying to keep track of all these plates? Sorry to say, but this looks like a weak attempt by Mormon to consolidate sets of plates. It's unclear, but Mormon says Amalecki's plates were given to King Benjamin, who put them with other plates, and they all made it into Mormon's hands far in the future. It would've been helpful if the author added better descriptors to these different plates, so we could tell them apart. And why is this time warp interruption even in here? Makes me wonder if the scribe was asking where these various story lines are going, and when will we ever get there?

Anyway, Mormon from the future assures us there are great things written on the plates and offers some more history of King Benjamin. The Lamanites came down and battled the Nephites again, and King Benjamin, with the sword of Laban, drove them out.

Some false Christs show up claiming to be the Messiah, false prophets and teachers too, but they're all rounded up and punished. King Benjamin reestablishes peace for the rest of his reign.

13

Book of Mosiah

Oops, we jump back to long books again. This one has twenty-nine chapters.

We pick up with King Benjamin, who now has three sons: Mosiah (not to be confused with the first King Mosiah), Helorum, and Helaman. Unfortunately, the over-the-top, verbose, rambling speeches return when King Benjamin addresses the people and announces his son Mosiah will take over as King. Benjamin also describes being visited by an angel who announces that Jesus Christ will be coming down to earth soon, birthed by his mother, Mary. Once he arrives, he'll perform miracles, provide salvation, get crucified, then rise from the dead. Lots of fire, brimstone, blood, religious rhetoric, yak, yak. King Mosiah takes over at age thirty. Benjamin lives three more years then dies. It's now 121 BC.

Remember those people that moved out of the land of Zarahemla into the wilderness a few generations ago, after the first King Mosiah? Well, new King Mosiah wonders what happened to them. Turns out they settled in the land of Lehi-

Nephi. The King sends out a search party led by Ammon. The searchers wander for forty days until they're taken prisoner by soldiers of King Limhi, who rules Lehi-Nephi. During their interrogation, King Limhi realizes that Ammon and the search party are from the Nephites, their old brethren.

King Limhi is thrilled. He explains how he and his people are being held in economic bondage by the Lamanites and have to pay a ridiculously high tax. He'd rather be slaves to the delightful Nephites than serve the filthy Lamanites.

It gets better—King Limhi's people discovered a huge destroyed civilization with skeletons, ruins, swords, armor, and, best of all, their history engraved on twenty-four golden plates! Unfortunately, Limhi couldn't translate the engravings on the plates. Does Ammon know anyone who could decipher the plates? Yessiree! King Mosiah owns special seer stones from God and can do it for sure! King Limhi declares that seers are even more exalted than prophets! (Nice pat on the back Joseph Smith, user of seer stones and prophet-in-residence, you're doubly awesome.)

Just when the story is getting good, a few chapters interrupt the timeline without explanation and serve us a tangent on how King Limhi's people ended up in bondage to the Lamanites. Hint: they transgressed, started drinking wine, playing the harlot, behaving badly, etc.

Oh, no, then the author lapses into Old Testament–type doom and gloom prophecy like we suffered through in Nephi 1 and 2. Then some New Testament–type verbiage: Father, Son, crucifixion, ascension into heaven. Oh, and a Mormon belief gets introduced—little kids get eternal life automatically, because they haven't been corrupted yet.

After this long digression, which we'll skip to keep our timeline on track, we finally get back to Ammon and King Limhi. The King and his people really want to get out from under Lamanite rule. So they come up with a plan. The Lamanite guards have a habit of drinking wine every night, so the King tells all the subjects to quietly pack their bags and sends extra wine one night to the sentries, who get so drunk they fall fast asleep. Then King Limhi, Ammon, and all the people sneak out the back gate of the city.

Ammon leads the group down to the land of Zarahemla, where the main body of Nephites then lived, and they are welcomed as new subjects of King Mosiah.

Oops, more historical digression and information about a belief sneaks in again out of nowhere. Another group, the followers of Alma, escape with God's help from the Lamanites and join up under King Mosiah too. Alma was a holy preacher and a strong proponent of full-body baptism as a way of creating a covenant between a believer and God. Before escaping he began this ritual in a pure pond known as the waters of Mormon. Later he continued baptizing in whatever water was available.

Mosiah 18

5 Now, there was in Mormon a fountain of pure water, and Alma resorted thither, there being near the water a thicket of small trees, where he did hide himself in the daytime from the searches of the king.

Mosiah 18

8 And it came to pass that he said unto them: Behold, here are the waters of Mormon (for thus were they called) and now, as ye are desirous to come into the fold of God ...

Mosiah 18

13 And when he had said these words, the Spirit of the Lord was upon him, and he said: Helam, I baptize thee, having authority from the Almighty God, as a testimony that ye have entered into a covenant to serve him until you are dead as to the mortal body; and may the Spirit of the Lord be poured out upon you; and may he grant unto you eternal life, through the redemption of Christ, whom he has prepared from the foundation of the world.

Now King Mosiah gathers the conglomeration of new and old Nephites together and brings them up to speed on their history. Even though the combined tribe is large, they're still outnumbered two to one by the Lamanites.

After King Mosiah speaks, Alma gives a religious presentation and baptizes many, including old King Limhi. King Mosiah grants Alma the power to ordain priests and establish church congregations throughout the lands. Things are good again, for a while.

Wouldn't you know it, the younger generation starts saying they don't really believe in baptism or the resurrection of the dead, and they'd rather not join the church, preferring to hang out and party instead. The ranks of these party people steadily grow.

Alma is not amused and drags the sinners before the King for a punishment decision. But King Mosiah punts it back to Alma. Naturally, Alma bumps it up to the Lord for a ruling.

The Lord weighs in with a long answer that basically gives Alma the priestly authority to forgive sins if the offender confesses and repents. Those who will not confess and repent are cast out of the church and God promises to send them directly to hell at the last judgment. (This "casting out" banishment is still threatened and used within the Mormon religion. It's a favorite of many religions and cults.)

Okay, glad we got that settled. Unbelievers start to multiply and persecute the good church people. Alma goes back to King Mosiah and has the King outlaw any hassling of churchgoers. Oh, and by the way, priests should work and not be supported by the people. (Another Mormon concept.)

Well, surprise shocker, Alma Jr. and the sons of King Mosiah come out publically as nonbelievers! Alma Jr. is a particularly vocal critic of the church. He is also wicked and happens to enjoy false idols. Yikes.

Things are so bad that an angel of the Lord intervenes by appearing to the miscreant boys and yelling at them with a thunderous voice. The angel reminds them of all the awesome things God has done for their people in the past. Alma Jr. is struck dumb and mute!

Alma Sr. gathers the high priests and they pray for two straight days. Miraculously, Alma Jr. is saved. He gets up, repents, and, along with King Mosiah's formerly juvenile delinquent sons, becomes a traveling salesman preacher for the church. Hallelujah!

Mosiah's sons are so born again, they ask King Mosiah

for permission to go up to the archenemy Lamanites, inform them just how rotten their ancestors were, and cure them of their hatred toward the Nephites, so then everyone could be friends. Kumbaya! King Mosiah asked the Lord about it and got a green light for the lads. You go, missionaries!

Meanwhile, King Mosiah had a project to do. He attached two seer stones to a wooden bow and used them as glasses to translate the golden plates brought by former King Limhi. These plates contained bad news about how that mystery civilization got destroyed—but we won't find out yet.

King Mosiah collects the brass plates, gold plates, plates of Nephi, the magic direction ball, and gives them to Alma Sr. to safeguard and hand down to posterity.

King Mosiah gets ready to retire, but all his sons are out trying to save the souls of the Lamanites, and he doesn't really trust them anyway; so he decides not to have a king and instead appoints judges (like in the Bible's Old Testament). These wise judges can enforce God's commandments on the population. This should work out better, and besides, getting rid of a future bad king is always a bloodbath. And we can even elect judges democratically—that should be great. And we can have appeals courts too. And it will be a land of liberty and equality, a veritable land of the free. And everyone can do his part! (Joseph Smith embraces some of these American concepts and frequently gets carried away with patriotic fervor.)

The people rejoice and elect Alma Sr. as the first judge. Justice and peace reign among the Nephites in the land of Zarahemla.

Alma Sr. and King Mosiah die, bringing us to the year 91 BC.

14

Book of Alma

Holy cow, sixty-three chapters—a new record for Joseph Smith, the human dictation machine. But guess what? It's now the character of Alma Jr. taking the helm as narrator. Alma Jr. is now the Chief Judge of the Nephites. (We'll refer to him as Alma, as this book does, since his dad, Alma Sr., is history.)

Alma's first case to decide as Chief Judge concerns the murder of a burly false prophet named Gideon. It came to pass that Gideon had been preaching that the people should financially support the priests, and that the good Lord created all men, so everyone will be saved on Judgment Day, no matter how they behaved—clearly a religious heresy. Gideon was gaining a loyal following, but then went full megachurch preacher and started wearing expensive clothes and jewelry, and probably a fancy haircut. One day he locked horns with an establishment priest, named Nehor, who pulled a knife and killed Gideon. Nehor is brought before Alma for judgment.

Alma denounces what Gideon was doing, calling it priestcraft: preaching for money and an extravagant lifestyle.

Yet what Nehor did was not cool, so he sentenced him to death.

False priestcraft scammers continued to be an annoyance throughout the land. Church priests who worked other jobs and lived modestly became very successful by following the rules.

Civil War

Five years into Alma's tenure, a cunning character named Amlici attracts a large group of supporters who want him to become not Chief Judge, but King!

The church is livid because, well, first, that's undemocratic, and second, they know Amlici will shut the church down! Public caucuses debate the issue and the majority vote "No King."

Amlici, being a political animal, incites his followers, now referred to as Amlicites, to take up weapons and rebel against their fellow Nephites. A big, bloody civil war occurs on the hill of Amnihu. Over 6,000 Nephites are killed, so the Lord strengthens them. They retaliate and 12,532 Amlicites are slaughtered and the remainder retreat.

Alma sends spies to follow them. The spies report that the surviving Amlicites have joined forces with a dark-skinned Lamanite army in the land of Minon!

Another huge battle occurs on the banks of the River Sidon. God again assists the Nephites. There's even a one-on-one sword duel between Alma and Amlici. Alma wins and kills Amlici. The combined Amlicite-Lamanite army flees. The Nephites chase them all the way to the wilderness of Hermounts, where ravenous beasts roam. Vultures and beasts devour them!

If that wasn't enough drama, another Lamanite army shows up ready to rumble. Alma, wounded from the sword duel, sends the Nephite army up to engage them, and with God's help they are victorious again.

The Lord is so ticked off he marks the rebellious Amlicites with a red splotch on their foreheads. This wasn't as bad as turning them completely dark red or black like the Lamanites, but it's explained that it will have the same effect of keeping the dark races from interbreeding with the lily-white, delightsome Nephites. And just so we're clear, all are reminded that any mingling of seed results in the same curse on all future descendants.

The Nephites bury their dead and try to recover. They get back to basics, the Church grows, and they have three years of peace under the judges.

Of course, trouble brews again as people start to accumulate wealth, fancy clothes, and pride. Alma definitely has a thing against costly apparel. Church attendance declines and income equality and wickedness return. Alma is tired, so he taps Nephihah to succeed him as Chief Judge, but Alma retains his job as the High Priest of the Church.

Road Trip
Alma then takes his show on the road, preaching the usual things throughout all the Nephite lands. One of those Nephite zones was the land of Mormon, where he established a church and baptized believers in the waters of Mormon like his father, Alma Sr., did before fleeing to join King Mosiah.

Many chapters of Alma's speeches follow. We do learn a few things: the son of God's bowels are full of mercy, and the filthy are doomed.

This portion resembles the New Testament's Acts of the Apostles, where Paul (in this case, Alma) travels around preaching. Things don't always go well. Alma strikes out in the city of Ammonihah, because Satan had gotten to the people first. Alma gets booted out. An angel appears and gives him a pep talk, telling Alma to remind the inhabitants that God will flame them if they don't listen. Alma goes back and recruits an assistant preacher, Amulek, but the citizens of Ammonihah still won't repent and try to toss them into jail, but an angel springs the two preachers free. (Just like Paul in the New Testament.)

We also hear a long discourse about the monetary currency of the realm and the salary of judges. The names of the various denominations are very creative: a senine, seon, limnah, or shum of gold; a senum, amnor, ezrom, or onti of silver; a shiblon is half a senum and equals a half measure of barley. This goes on and on and becomes the basis of a theological and fiscal public debate between Amulek and a slippery lawyer, Zeezrom. Amulek wins when he deftly catches Zeezrom in a lie. Zeezrom trembles.

Some of the debate spectators repent. Others are angry and tie Alma and Amulek up with cords. Zeezrom sees the light and tries to defend them but the crowd spits on him. The judge of the city (who was an old buddy of Nehor) casts out and exiles any man who believes in God, rounds up their wives and children, and burns the families alive while Alma and Amulek are forced to watch. The judge spanks Alma and Amulek on the cheeks in public, then imprisons them. Dang, that's one mean judge.

A few weeks later, all the local judges of Ammonihah visit the jail and taunt Alma and Amulek, "Where's your God now boys?" The two prisoners stand and pray, and God lets them break the cords that bound them and causes the entire prison to collapse, killing everyone except Alma and Amulek, who escape unscathed!

Alma and Amulek hit the road and land in Sidon. There they meet all the faithful men who got booted out of the last town and also the sleazy lawyer Zeezrom, who is burning up with fever in bed and wants to repent and accept Christ as his personal savior. The boys make this happen and baptize Zeezrom, who miraculously springs out of bed and busts some dance moves right there! Many converts are baptized too and a church is established in Sidon.

Lamanites Again
The judges have now been in charge of the Nephites for eleven years. It's now 80 BC.

Multiple Lamanite armies descend on the Nephite territory. One army attacks those stiffnecked nonbelievers in Ammonihah and destroy the city, wiping out every last Ammonihahite (sounds like a type of chemical). Dogs eat their dead carcasses. The other armies drag captives from surrounding Nephite areas and take them into the wilderness. (Nothing good can happen there!)

The Nephite army has gotten complacent and isn't ready to fight. Chief Captain Zoram asks Alma to get some advice from God. The Lord sends the Nephite troops to the edge of the wilderness and they rescue every single one of the captives. The Lamanites retreat for three more years.

Sons of Mosiah

Remember Mosiah's three unruly sons who repented and went off to try to convert the Lamanites? Well, here's what happened. They split up and ministered to the ferocious Lamanites for fourteen years.

The oldest son, Ammon, went into the Lamanite land settled by the sons of Ishmael, who were part of Lehi's original trans-Atlantic sailors. As soon as Ammon arrived, the Lamanites tied him up and brought him before their King Lamoni. Ammon became a servant to the King, and his reputation soared when he defended the King's flock of sheep by cutting off the arms of some bully Lamanites who were harassing them. Ammon used the power of God and the sword of Ammon to lop off the limbs.

King Lamoni supposed that Ammon was the Great Spirit whom the Lamanites were expecting. Ammon gains the King's trust and informs him about God, the coming of Christ, and history from the time of Adam and Eve up to the present. King Lamoni believes it all and falls into a deep coma lasting two days. Everyone thought he was dead, and he even started to stinketh!

Ammon predicts the King will wake on the third day and become a believer—and it happens! Multitudes are converted and start a church. Remember, God will save anyone who repents and joins up, even Lamanites. Many people still don't buy it and murmur against Ammon.

King Lamoni is now fully recovered and a true believer. God tells Ammon that his brother Aaron is being held prisoner in the Lamanite-occupied land of Middoni. King Lamoni offers to help because he's friendly with Middoni's King Antiomno.

Lamoni and Ammon head out in horse-drawn chariots.

They successfully free Aaron and his crew, who are in rough shape. We then hear about Aaron's preaching attempts to stiffnecked Lamanite groups such as Amalekites, Amulonites, and inhabitants of the village Ani-Anti, where they were taken prisoner.

Soon after his release, Aaron converts King Lamoni's father, who is overall king of the entire Lamanite empire. It's a similar story where the empire King falls into a coma upon hearing about Christ's future arrival, then Aaron wakes him and he promptly converts. The King proclaims that all Lamanites should heed the words of Aaron and Ammon.

Geography

We then get a geography lesson about the different territories in the area. We still aren't told whether the stories are set in North, or Central, or South America (and many current Mormon theories abound).

We're told of a sea east and a sea west on each side of the continent. There's the wilderness area, and the River Sidon separating the Nephites from the Lamanites. Other new regions and cities are mentioned, like Bountiful, Desolation, and Jerusalem. It's not clear, but borders seem to shift constantly, and actual locations are vague and amorphous. A map would certainly help, but one is not offered.

More Conversions

Lamanites all over the place are laying down their weapons and accepting religion. Except for the Amalekites and Amulonites.

The converted kings of the Lamanites thought, "Hey,

our people need a new name." So they decided to now call themselves Anti-Nephi-Lehis. "Don't call us Lamanites anymore." These new converts prospered and shook off the curse of God. (But their skin didn't get any lighter.)

The unconverted Lamanites didn't like this turn of events, so they started planning a rebellion. To make matters worse, the recently converted King changed his name to King Anti-Nephi-Lehi. (Sorry readers.) The new King makes another dumb decision; he's embraced religion and nonviolence, so he instructs his followers to bury their swords in the dirt, and they do!

When the rebel Lamanite army shows up, the Anti-Nephi-Lehis come out of their city and lay down on the ground praising the Lord. The rebel army slays 1,500 of them, but then the soldiers start to feel bad about it. They start thinking there must be something to this religion stuff, and multitudes start converting right there!

The only soldiers not accepting God continue to be those hard-hearted Amelekites, Amulonites, and former followers of Nehor. They were so mad that they withdrew and went over to the land of Ammonihah, where they wiped out the population. Then they continued to battle against Nephites, wherever they found them.

Migration, Time to Move

The Lamanites, now mostly angry Amalekites, still enjoyed harassing the Anti-Nephi-Lehis. So Ammon asked King Anti-Nephi-Lehi if he'd consider moving the population to a new neighborhood. The King said to ask God. When Ammon did, God said, "That's a great idea." So the King agreed. All the Anti-Nephi-Lehis started a mass migration down to the land of Zarahemla, where the Nephites lived. When they got to the strip of wilderness separating the two lands, Ammon said, "Wait here and I'll go ask the Nephites if they want new roommates."

Ammon meets up with his old pal Alma, who is so overjoyed in God that he passes out temporarily! Anyway, the Nephites are thrilled to accept the Anti-Nephi-Lehis, even though they're former Lamanites, but now they love God too.

The Nephites give them the nice land of Jershon, over by the East Sea, which has a relaxing water view. And since the Anti-Nephi-Lehis are staunch pacifists, the Nephite armies are repositioned on the borders to protect them. The Nephites have only one condition for their new guests—they insist they change that ridiculous name, Anti-Nephi-Lehi, and instead call them the people of Ammon. Everybody, including me, is happy about that.

Not Another Battle
Yes, another battle occurs, but this one is described as the biggest battle to occur since Lehi and his gang landed their boat in the New World.

The armies of the Lamanites attack the Nephites and renamed people of Ammon. Huge casualties occur on each side, with heaps of dead bodies and lots of mourning, but the good guys seem to prevail by 76 BC.

An Antichrist
After everyone recovers, the Nephites in the land of Zarahemla, and their neighbors the people of Ammon in the land of

Jershon, had some peace for a year or so, until it came to pass that a dude named Korihor shows up and starts preaching that there's no redeemer coming: "You guys are fools, why are you burdening yourselves? You just believe this stuff because your forefathers did—it's all just the product of deranged minds." (Author's note: maybe he's on to something.) For these proclamations, Korihor is labeled the Antichrist.

The narrator informs us that there's no law saying you have to believe everything, because this land is sort of a liberal democracy, with a king, but Korihor starts to gain a following. Wickedness and whoredoms quickly return, as expected with such heretical teachings.

Korihor is called out by a high priest, Giddonah, and they debate. The Antichrist Korihor makes some solid points, but Giddonah orders him tied up and sent to Alma and the Chief Judge for trial.

Korihor acts as his own attorney at the trial. Alma interrogates him, but the prisoner sticks to his story. Alma warns him to give up, or God will smite thee really bad. Korihor says there is no God and challenges Alma for a sign proving there is. With Alma's clever trap set, Korihor is struck dumb and mute! (Didn't we see this happen before?)

Korihor scribbles a note explaining that the devil made him do it. See, the devil appeared to him disguised as an angel and told him what to say—oh, and can you waive this penalty and un-mute me please?

Sorry, no such luck. Releasing him, Alma tells him that he'd probably just sin again if he had a voice. So Korihor wanders around the town as a beggar and is later trampled to death by a mob of Zoramites. Lesson: religious crime just doesn't pay.

Zoramites

Since we just heard about the Zoramites, followers of Zoram, how about a story? Alma hears that they're perverting the Lord's message, and Zoram, their leader, is making them worship dumb idols. The Zoramites had previously split off from the Nephites and lived in the land of Antionum, south of Jershon, over by the wilderness where the Lamanites lived.

Alma heads over there with the religious posse of Aaron, Ammon, Zeezrom (I call him Double Z), some sons, and others to check it out.

When they arrive, they find the perversion worse than advertised—the Zoramites had built synagogues and proclaimed that they are the chosen people! They loved gold and fine clothing, went to synagogue once a week, and forgot about God the other six days. Oh, and there's no Christ either.

Alma and his crew are aghast! They start praying furiously for the Zoramites' souls. When they try to enter the synagogues, the bouncers refuse to let them in because their clothes aren't nice enough: "Yo, there's a dress code here."

So, Alma and his helpers preach to the subclass of less affluent Zoramites, who were also not cool enough to get into the synagogues. This hits a nerve. They're told that being poor is a blessed thing. Next, we are given a parable about seeds. More speeches from Alma's posse follow for many, many chapters. The crowd is hooked. They convert and move to Jershon to join the people of Ammon.

The upper-class Zoramites are mad. All their domestic help just left town. The Zoramite lawyers send menacing letters to Jershon demanding the poor Zoramites be returned forthwith. No way, fat cats, is the response.

So the rich, angry Zoramites plot to join with the filthy Lamanites and prepare to attack the people of Ammon in Jershon.

The people of Ammon retreat to the land of Melek and leave Jershon to the Nephite army to defend.

Pass the Plates

Wait, before we get to the next battle, Alma passes the various sets of plates, and the direction ball and compass, on to his son Helaman, after a long speech of course. Then comes a speech to son Shiblon, who is sent out with Helaman to preach.

Then we learn of a sitdown with his underachiever son, Corianton. Alma lays out his disappointment that Corianton didn't go into the family business of preaching like his brothers. Instead, he went to the land of Sidon, over near the Lamanites' zone, where he fell in love with a harlot named Isabelle.

Lust is a serious carnal abomination, he is told. Then Alma blames him for losing all those Zoramites that Alma failed to convert, because they saw Corianton carousing around. Guilt-trip anyone? Then Corianton gets a multichapter lecture on eternal damnation and everything else we've already heard over and over. You're on your last leg, Sonny, so better repent and join me and your brothers preaching.

Back to the War

Recall that the upper class Zoramites joined up with the Lamanites. The leader of the alliance is Zerahemnah, and he appointed the meanest Amalakites he could find as military commanders. Their goal was to turn the combined Nephites and the former Anti-Nephi-Lehis, now called people of

Ammon, into their slaves, and maybe throw in some spankings too.

The sides assemble to rumble. The Nephite commander is the twenty-five-year-old Moroni, who decks out the Nephites in the latest military protective technology—armor breastplates, shields, and thick clothing.

When the nearly naked Lamanites see this gear, they panic and haul butt into the wilderness. Moroni sends spies to track them and asks God to provide satellite surveillance. He learns the Lamanites are moving against the unsuspecting people of Manti instead. Moroni leaves a reserve force to protect the Nephites, moves the bulk of his forces to areas around the west bank of the river Sidon, and rallies the people of Manti to join him.

The Lamanites attack near the hill of Riplah and are surrrounded by armored Nephites in a valley near the river. The usual bloodbath ensues. Both sides suffer huge losses, but the poorly equipped Lamanites take the worst of it. Moroni maneuvers his legions and surrounds the Lamanites again.

Just before slaughtering them, Moroni calls a timeout. He tells the Lamanite commander Zerahemna, "Look, God is clearly on the Nephites' side, so surrender and we'll let you all go if you promise not to war with us again." General Zerahemna bows down and says, "We'll give up our weapons, but we can't promise not to fight in the future, you know we are Lamanites after all."

Moroni gives Zerahemna and his men their swords and weapons back, but insists they make the promise. Zerahemna gets mad, picks up his sword, and charges Moroni. One of Moroni's soldiers intervenes and actually scalps General

Zerahemna (just like in those nineteenth-century accounts about Indians!). He then hoists the scalp up on the end of his sword. Zerahemna, minus his scalp, runs out of there.

Moroni offers the same deal to all the Lamanite troops. Many say, "Sounds good to us. We promise we won't attack again." They take their weapons and streak into the wilderness.

Other Lamanite warriors are furious that Moroni had their boss scalped in public and refuse to make the promise. So Moroni orders his men to start slaying them. Zerahemna, watching from a safe distance, yells to Moroni: "Okay, you win. We promise not to have another war. Just let my guys go." Moroni agrees, and the surviving Lamanite fighters sprint to the wilderness.

Clean-up time again. The Nephite army dumps the corpses into the river Sidon one more time and goes home.

Alma's Exit Interview
It's about 73 BC and since it's highly unlikely Alma could top that spectacular battle as his grand finale, his son Helaman starts narrating and engraving history on the plates.

On his first day on the job, Helaman learns of a secret prophecy from Alma, which he is not to tell anyone. Four hundred years after Jesus shows up, the wonderful Nephites will fall into disbelief. There'll be wars, famines, pestilence, and bloodshed, and the Nephites will go extinct! A few Nephites will become disciples of God, but any other survivors will become Lamanites.

Alma then disappears. It's explained that he may have been taken up to God by the Spirit, or buried by God himself. Holy mackerel!

More Drama

Helaman takes over from Alma and starts preaching. Trouble begins right away. A big brute, Amalickiah, wants to be named king, and he has many supporters called Amalickiahites (naturally).

Moroni, leader of the Nephite armies, gets wind of this and inspires the Nephites by ripping a piece of his coat, writing "Title of Liberty" on it, sticking it on a pole, and waving it around. This works and Moroni gathers a crowd even bigger than Amalickiah's.

The Amalickiahites realize they're outnumbered and shuffle off toward the wilderness. Before they go, Moroni offers them the same deal as the Lamanites. Many Amalickiahites agree and promise to be peaceful, but some, along with their leader, refuse and leave to join forces with the Lamanites in the wilderness.

Amalickiah finagles, through treachery, to become a Lamanite army officer. He poisons the top general and takes over their army. He then orchestrates the murder of the King of the Lamanites, blames it on the King's servants, marries the Queen, and usurps the throne as King of the Lamanites.

Under new King Amalickiah, the Lamanites become more wicked, ferocious, nonreligious, and generally disagreeable. Amalickiah's first order of business is to incite his population against the Nephites. He employs minions to give incendiary speeches from the city's towers, and appoints ruthless Zoramites as army captains. The legions prepare to move against the Nephites.

Moroni senses trouble and deploys his troops to fortify the Nephite villages. He preaches liberty and freedom, and refers to the Nephites as Christians. Helaman baptizes new followers.

Behold, yea, the Lamanite army attacks the city of Ammonihah with arrows and rocks, but they're no match for the dirt ridges the Nephites cleverly built up around the city limits. Oh, wait, Joseph Smith is caught on a technicality: wasn't Ammonihah destroyed previously? Well, yes, but part of it was rebuilt. That's why the Lamanites attacked it; they thought it would be an easy victory. Okay, we can continue now my pesky scribe.

Even though the Lamanites and Amalickiahites are now better outfitted with thick animal skin uniforms and breastplates, they can't overcome Moroni's ingenious defense of a dirt wall around the city. The attackers retreat and march toward the land of Noah to try another offensive.

Oh, no, Noah is protected by an even better dirt wall! Lamanites savagely attack again and are repulsed. They decide to try to dig the walls down but are slaughtered by the Nephite defenders' arrows and hurled rocks. The Nephite commander, Lehi (now we're recycling more names!), scores a defensive victory. All the Zoramite captains are slain along with one thousand of their soldiers. The Nephites, clothed with armor, shields, and—a new addition to their kit—head plates, suffer no fatalities.

The Lamanite survivors limp back home. When they get back, they have to tell King Amalickiah, and he goes ballistic, cursing God and vowing to drink Moroni's blood!

Moroni, the great tactician, continues fortifying Nephite settlements. He constructs timber walls and adds pickets on top of the dirt walls and erects watchtowers.

Chief Captain Moroni sends an army to clear the eastern wilderness of Lamanites, successfully achieving manifest destiny by securing Nephite lands from the East Sea all the way to the West Sea. Nephites create new towns occupying the land. The sparkling new city of Moroni and the cities of Aaron and Lehi are started in the land Nephihah. Prosperity reigns and everyone becomes rich, proving God is real. This lasts about four years.

An internal skirmish with the people of Morianton is squelched by Moroni. Chief Judge Nephihah dies and is replaced by his son Pahoran.

A group of upper-class rich guys challenge Pahoran to change the laws and allow institution of a king and noblemen. They're called King-men, and Pahoran refuses to give in. The Lamanite army moves to the Nephite borders, so Moroni orders a military draft. The King-men are angry and refuse to be drafted into the army. Moroni backs up Pahoran and orders the army to kill four thousand of the draft-dodging King-men. The rest are thrown in prison and there's no time for niceties like trials.

Lamanite forces attack and take the not-yet finished city of Moroni. King Amalickiah's Lamanite armies capture multiple Nephite cities along the eastern seaboard. The Lamanites then march to the outskirts of the Nephi land Bountiful. A strong Nephite army, led by Teancum (who had successfully put down the Morianton insurrection), gets ready to confront them. While both armies are camped, Teancum sneaks into the sleeping Lamanite King Amalickiah's tent and silently spears him with a javelin to the heart! Then he escapes back to his camp.

When the Lamanites discover this assassination, they retreat to the city of Mulek. Amalickiah's brother, Ammoron, is appointed King. (Something tells me Ammoron did not have an easy time in school.) King Ammoron and some guards head back to his capital to inform the queen of Amalickiah's death. Both armies take the opportunity to reinforce.

Military Tactics

Moroni is reticent to attack the Lamanites in the fortified city of Mulek, so he devises a decoy plan to draw them out. Teancum approaches the city with a small force. Sensing an easy win, the Lamanite army comes out to smote them. Meanwhile, Chief Captain Moroni is hiding in the woods with a full-strength army. Teancum retreats, leading the Lamanite troops far away from the safety of the city.

Moroni splits his force, sending half to capture the now lightly defended city of Mulek, and the other half after the Lamanite army that's chasing the decoy Teancum. The city quickly surrenders. Teancum lures the Lamanites, under the command of Jacob, into a trap near the land Bountiful. They're surrounded by Nephite armies led by Lehi and Moroni. Chief Captain Moroni offers them a chance to surrender—some accept, but many don't. Jacob tries to fight his way back to Mulek and is killed. Surviving Lamanites are taken prisoner and marched to Bountiful. There they are put to work constructing a dirt wall topped by timbers around the city.

Moroni gives the city of Mulek to his Captain Lehi as a prize.

Prisoner Swap?

King Ammoron sends a note to Chief Captain Moroni suggesting a prisoner exchange. Moroni mulls it over, but since the dastardly Lamanites have taken women and children prisoner, in addition to soldiers, he writes back saying for each Lamanite soldier exchanged he wants a Nephite soldier plus a wife and kids. Then Moroni adds in a bunch of nasty, unnecessary comments like, "Oh, and by the way, you're a child from hell." This does not help.

Ammoron writes back, "Hey, I haven't forgotten that you just murdered my brother Amalickiah, and while we're at it, your forefathers screwed over my forefathers Laman and Lemuel and the sons of Ishmael. I'll agree to the prisoner exchange if you disarm, so will we, and we can end this bloody war. How about it?" Then he throws in an unnecessary: "And you really don't know there is a God. But if there is one, he made us all, didn't he?" Signed, King Ammoron.

Moroni reads this epistle and is even more incensed. "Forget it, deal's off!"

Moroni concocts a scheme to steal the Nephite prisoners back. He finds a direct descendant of Laman, named Laman, who hates King Ammoron. He assembles a stealth special forces team to infiltrate the guards who watched over the Nephite prisoners in the city of Gid. Laman and his commandos give the Lamanite guards a supply of wine, which they happily chug. That night, the drunken guards fall into a deep sleep (yet another repeat story). While they're passed out, Moroni sneaks weapons to the prisoners, even the women and children! Then his armies surround the city.

When the Lamanites wake up, they're stunned to see

their city of Gid surrounded and the Nephite prisoners inside holding weapons, even the toddlers! The entire city surrenders. Moroni has worked a bloodless coup d'état, because he doesn't wish to kill unnecessarily. The Nephite prisoners are freed and relocated to the city of Bountiful.

The Lamanites supposedly tried the same tricks on the Nephites, but the Nephites were far too smart for them.

Helaman Update

Moroni receives an epistle from Helaman with news from his area. Remember the nonviolent people of Ammon who joined the Nephites? Well, they have upheld their oath of pacifism, but their sons are tired of persistent Lamanite harassment and attacks. So two thousand of the sons have taken up arms and declared Helaman their leader. These new warriors joined the depleted ranks of local Nephite ruler Antipus in the city of Judea.

The Lamanites had successfully occupied some cities in the land of Manti. Helaman relates a very similar war story using his two thousand "sons" to lure the Lamanite army out of their stronghold city and into a battle with Antipus's Nephite army. It's basically the same plot with some minor differences. Antipus gets killed. The two thousand sons fight valiantly and suffer zero casualties because of their strong belief in God. The Lamanite army is defeated; many are taken prisoner, others are slain.

You've got mail. Helaman receives an epistle letter from Lamanite King Ammoron. The King offers to trade the Lamanite city of Antiparah for the return of the soldiers taken prisoner.

Helaman replies, "No; we think we can take the town by force, so we'll just keep the prisoners, thank you." Helaman's army approaches Antiparah and the Lamanites flee. That worked out.

Next, Helaman surrounded and starved out the Lamanite-occupied city of Cumeni.

By now, Helaman had so many prisoners that it was hard to guard them all. So, he had two thousand of them killed. (Wow, how did God feel about that?) The rest of the prisoners he shipped back to the Nephite land of Zarahemla. On the way, there's a prisoner uprising; many are killed and a bunch escape.

Helaman then lays siege upon the city of Manti. The Lamanites wised up and didn't fall for the decoy trick again. This city was a much tougher nut to crack. So the Nephites prayed extra hard. God helped them with a redundant plan.

A small contingent of Helaman's troops camped outside the city walls near the border of the wilderness. Two larger Nephite divisions hid in the bushes. The Lamanites saw that Helaman's group was small, so they sent their entire force out to destroy them. Helaman's small group retreated into the wilderness. When the Lamanite army passed by the two hidden Nephite divisions, the two divisions swept into the city and overpowered the few guards.

The Lamanites continued chasing Helaman's group through the wilderness until nightfall, then stopped to camp. In a bold move, Hellman marched his small group without sleep, through the night and back around to the city of Manti, where his other troops opened the door and let them in.

The next day the Lamanites resumed the hunt but

couldn't find any Nephites, so they returned to Manti. They were shocked when they saw that Helaman and the Nephites now held the town! Demoralized, the Lamanites completely abandoned the area and returned home, but on their way they stole many women and children.

Before ending his report to Moroni, Helaman complains about the lack of government support and cuts to the defense budget.

Back to Moroni
Moroni was overjoyed to hear of Helaman's success in regaining Nephite cities. He wrote to Chief Judge Pahoran requesting that troops and supplies be sent to Helaman. Moroni realized it's easier to reinforce the cities than to lose them and have to retake them from the rotten Lamanites again.

No sooner had he mailed his letter than he learned the Lamanites had conquered the city Nephihah, in Moroni's neck of the woods.

Moroni wrote again to the government boss man Pahoran down in Zarahemla, accusing him and the bureaucracy of neglecting the armies. "Freedom isn't free; support the troops. We're getting constantly barraged up here on the borderlands. You guys in the bloated government are getting slothful. Our blood is going to be on your heads. And don't get me started on those King-men! You'd better send supplies to me and Helaman, or I will personally come down there and smite your behind!" Sincerely, Moroni, Chief Captain of the Army.

Insurrection
Pahoran writes back immediately informing Moroni that the

King-men have staged a rebellion and driven Pahoran from the city Zarahemla. He's in exile in the land of Gideon with as many supporters as he can muster. The rebels have appointed a king, Pachus, and they have a big following. They've also formed an unholy alliance with Lamanite King Ammoron! Ammoron has promised them Zarahemla, in exchange for all other Nephite territories, which would become Lamanite immediately!

Pahoran says he's tried to send aid to the armies, but the King-men blocked it. He asks Moroni to come meet him in Gideon with some soldiers. "Put Lehi and Teancum in charge up there and get down here fast. And it was good hearing from you." Your friend, Pahoran, recently deposed Chief Judge and Governor.

Moroni marches toward Gideon with a small squad, flying the Liberty flag. Along the way, thousands take up swords and join him.

Within two verses, Moroni joins up with Pahoran, marches on Zarahemla, kills King Pachus, takes the King-men into custody, and restores Pahoran to power.

The King-men receive fair trials and are executed for high treason, without lengthy appeals.

Moroni orders reinforcements and supplies to Helaman, Lehi, and Teancum. Then he marches with Pahoran and soldiers to try to retake the city of Nephihah from the Lamanites. Moroni executes a nighttime stealth climb up the city walls, then has his men rappel down ropes to open the city gates from the inside, silently letting the army in. When the Lamanite troops wake up, they freak out and run away from the city. This time, Moroni orders his men to pursue, allowing them to kill fleeing Lamanites and take others prisoner. By taking Nephihah, Moroni also liberates Nephite prisoners and adds them to his army.

Moroni and Pahoran chase the Lamanites from city to city, kicking ass the whole way. Moroni's army links up with Lehi and Teancum's forces and drive the running Lamanites to the land of Moroni, where the main Lamanite army, under the command of King Ammoron, is positioned against the wilderness border.

Everyone rests for the night, except Teancum, who has unresolved anger toward the enemy. Teancum sneaks into the Lamanite camp and spears King Ammoron in the heart with a javelin. (Sounds vaguely familiar.) Before dying, King Ammoron yells for help and Teancum is captured and killed. (Oh, it's slightly different.)

Teancum is remembered as a true son of liberty. The Nephite army attacks the Lamanites, slaughtering many and driving the rest out of the land.

Wrap Up
Moroni refortifies Nephite areas and retires from the military, giving command of the armies to his son, Moronihah. Pahoran returns to Chief Judgeship. Helaman gets the church going again, then dies. The Nephites prosper, multiply, and grow rich again.

Shiblon takes possession of the plates and sacred stuff. Moroni dies. The Lamanites attack again and Moronihah drives them back. Shiblon dies and passes the stuff to Helaman's son, oddly enough named Helaman.

It is now around the year 50 something BC.

In an unusual end passage, a curious man named Hagoth builds a huge ship on the West Sea and dispatches a large group of Nephites northward. An old character, Corianton, sails a ship laden with supplies north for the people. Hagoth builds other ships, fills them with men, women, and children and sends them northward. One ship is never heard from again; all passengers are presumed to have drowned in the deep West Sea. Another ship set sail and where it went, no one knows to this day.

A land-based migration of Nephites also occurs to the land northward.

Thus ends the Book of Alma, the longest book in the Book of Mormon.

15

Book of Helaman

Helaman, the son of Helaman, who was the son of Alma (who was of course the son of Alma), takes over as narrator. Pahoran, the reinstalled Chief Judge, dies and a fight breaks out over who will succeed him. It's a three-way election contest between Pahoran's son Pahoran, Paanchi, and Pacumeni. (Which sounds like a Mormon circus act.)

Pahoran Jr. wins and becomes Chief Judge. Pacumeni accepts the result. Paanchi and his supporters do not and incite a rebellion. Paanchi is quickly arrested and sentenced to death for obstructing liberty. His campaign workers are furious and send an assassin, Kishkumen, who murders Pahoran Jr. as he sits on his judge's throne and successfully escapes!

Second-place finisher Pacumeni takes over.

Hang on, the Lamanites raise a massive army now equipped with armor, shields, and brand-spanking-new head plates. They descend, led by Coriantumr, a fallen Nephite, and wage war. King Ammoron's son, Tubaloth, is now King of the Lamanites.

The Nephites have been so obsessed by their own political drama that they failed to post guards, and the Lamanite army marches right through the heartland and into the capital city of Zarahemla! Lamanite Commander Coriantumr slays thousands and personally smites the new Chief Judge Pacumeni, who was just sworn in. Adios Pacu, we hardly knew ye.

Coriantumr boldly continues marching right through the center of Nephite territory, laying waste. Nephite Chief Captain Moronihah had his forces arrayed far out on the borders and scrambled to intercept the Lamanite armies in the central regions. Moronihah catches them and bloody battles ensue. Coriantumr is killed and Moronihah retakes all the Nephite territory, including Zarahemla. Lamanite prisoners are sent home by Moronihah.

Back to Politics
Helaman Jr. (our narrator) is elected to the vacant Chief Judge position. The assassin, Kishkumen, is still at large. He reunites with the disgruntled losers of the last election, who are now led by a smooth-talking criminal named Gadianton. They plot to gain access to Helaman through a servant. Little do they know, the servant is a double agent loyal to Helaman. The servant leads Kishkumen into the judge's chamber where he plans to assassinate Helaman. Surprise—instead the servant stabs Kishkumen right in the heart! Plot foiled. Gadianton and his band bolt into the wilderness.

Joseph Smith gives us a little foreshadowing, explaining that Gadianton will become a central figure in the ultimate destruction of the Nephites at the end of this book—not the Book of Helaman, but the whole entire book. Stay tuned.

Northern Movement

Things quiet down for a few years. During this time, more and more Nephites migrate northward to settle the lands. Their predecessors, who sailed in the large ships built by Hagoth, had cut all the trees down, so the land is called Desolate. The new migrants are resourceful and build cement houses, since there is no wood. Manifest destiny is now fully achieved north to south, east to west. Shipping becomes big business.

Joseph Smith explains we don't really have time to go into these records. Let's get back to the Nephites.

Back to Zarahemla

Helaman Jr. proves to be a good, stable leader. He has two sons, Nephi and Lehi (now we've definitely run out of new names).

Things are peaceful. Gadianton relocated from the wilderness and is now lurking around in the suburbs. The church expands. God opens the door of heaven. Prosperity returns and the faithful grow rich and start to become uppity, boasting and prideful again, which is a recurring evil.

In 39 BC Helaman Jr. dies and his son Nephi becomes Chief Judge. Internal church arguments start flaring up with violence. Many Nephites defect and join the Lamanites. Once with them, they rile up the Lamanites enough to send an army down and capture all the lands of Zarahemla again.

Moronihah and the Nephite army are driven back into the land Bountiful. There they establish a defensive line. Over the next few years, Moronihah retakes about half their territory, but things are rather bleak.

It's explained that this setback was obviously because the Nephites had slacked off on their faith, enjoyed their riches, and stopped taking care of the poor. Oh, and some murdering, lying, plundering, and adultery didn't help either.

Moronihah, Nephi, and Lehi convince most people to repent, but it's getting to be a lost cause. They're outnumbered by the Lamanites and just hoping to hold onto their land. Wickedness is more prevalent, the church and belief are dwindling, laws are being corrupted, and most folks become obstinate and stiffnecked.

Nephi is bummed. He gives up his Chief Judge seat to Cezoram so he can join brother Lehi to preach full time and try to turn things around. They hit the road and preach to Nephites and convert Lamanites who occupy Zarahemla.

The boys even enter the Lamanite homeland to preach, but they're tossed into jail. While in the prison exercise yard, Nephi and Lehi are suddenly surrounded by a burning ring of fire! (Sorry, Johnny Cash.) The Lamanites and other prisoners are amazed. A dark cloud covers the yard and the earth rumbles. A voice from the sky says, "Repent y'all." All three hundred prisoners and guards are petrified. They repent and the ring of fire encircles the entire group. The heavens open and the Holy Spirit gives each man the gift of oratory. A voice commands them, "Now all y'all go forth and preach."

They do indeed go forth and convert the majority of the Lamanites, who disarm and give the Nephites all their land back!

A complete reversal: the Lamanites are now more righteous than the Nephites, who had mostly fallen into disbelief and wickedness. Many Lamanites move to Zarahemla and the northern territories to try to convince the Nephites to repent for cryin' out loud.

Since the Lamanites weren't warlike anymore, peace finally had a chance. Everyone, Lamanites and Nephites, grew rich in precious metals.

A few years later, envy and hoarding of riches leads to theft, corruption, and financial shenanigans. This is the perfect environment for the robber Gadianton and his crew to prosper. They murder Cezoram, and when his son is elevated to Chief Judge, they murder him too!

The mostly good Lamanites try to improve things and to apprehend Gadianton, but fail. Satan shows up and convinces most Nephites to join up with Gadianton! Gadianton promises them political appointments to cushy government jobs. They develop secret signs, words, handshakes, and covenants with Satan. In case you're wondering, it's explained this is the same Satan who tempted Eve in the Garden of Eden, plotted with her son Cain, and designed the Tower of Babel!

Gadianton and the wicked Nephites take over the entire government. Even God shuns the Nephites and starts to embrace the Lamanites.

Return of Nephi

Nephi comes back from the northland, having completely struck out trying to preach to the Nephites who migrated there.

When he sees that the robbers of Gadianton have taken over and corrupted everything, he's shattered. He goes up into a tower and wails, praying to God. A crowd of Nephites gather and he exhorts them to repent already! God's going to turn you into meat for beasts and dogs.

The local corrupt judges hear of this and urge the people

to seize Nephi and bring him to trial for speaking against the state. Nephi gives a long, fiery, prophetlike speech and at the end drops a bombshell—current Chief Judge Seezoram has been murdered!

Here's a prophecy that the crowd can actually fact check. They run over to the courthouse and, sure enough, the Chief Judge is lying in a puddle of blood, dead right there.

Whoa! Nephi must be a real prophet! The local judges see it quite differently—Nephi is a co-conspirator in the murder, that's how he knew about it—and they lock him up. Nephi's put on trial and gives inspiring testimony, including another prophecy. He tells them to go check out Seantum, the murdered judge's brother, and ask if he did it. Nephi predicts he'll deny it, but adds that if they check his coat, they'll find some blood. Seantum will then turn pale and confess.

And that's exactly what happens! Some people claim Nephi is a God, others say a true prophet. No matter, both are really good titles and he beats the rap.

Nephi is walking home from court when he hears a voice. It's God telling him he's blessed forever and doing a fine job. God gives Nephi the power to seal people and things together and also to cut them loose. Furthermore, he gets awarded the power to flatten mountains, if he feels like it, and is told to please warn the people they're going to be smitten soon if things don't improve.

Nephi is so psyched, he doesn't go home. Instead he starts preaching right away. "Repent or be destroyed."

Remarkably, even after he solved the crime of the century, the people don't buy Nephi's message. The corrupt robbers of Gadianton are still in charge, civil war skirmishes break out, and the people are still a mess.

Nephi pitches an idea to God: since the threat of being smitten really didn't get any traction among the population, how about a famine to get their attention?! God agrees and casts a multiyear great famine and drought upon the whole earth. Thousands die.

The survivors implore Nephi to intercede with God, so he prays for the famine and drought to end. It works and God sends rain and food. The people recover, the Church rebounds, Nephites and Lamanites live in peace for a year, and the robbers of Gadianton go underground (temporarily).

Yearly back and forth periods of belief and unbelief and intermittent clashes with the robbers continue. By 6 BC, it's getting exceedingly tiresome to hear about, Mr. Joseph Smith. (I'll spare you poor readers the ebb and flow of events, but it's pretty monotonous.) Generally, things slide toward evil.

This book desperately needs a new character—oh, here's one, Samuel the Lamanite prophet shows up and preaches to the Nephites. The Lamanites are following God's commandments; Nephites are getting progressively more wicked.

Samuel's message is to the point: repent, or God will shun you Nephites for four hundred years, then destroy you with pestilence, famine, and the sword. Don't procrastinate. God's not kidding this time.

Samuel continues, "Here's some good news for you people—in about five years the son of God is coming to redeem all the believers. Here's an unmistakable sign too—there will be a superbright light in the sky for two continuous days, followed by a new brilliant star the night before he shows up."

And there's more: Jesus Christ, the son of God, must die to save mankind, and then rise from the dead soon after so the dead can be saved. The signs will be (mostly) unmistakable. When he dies the earth will fall completely dark for about three days, until he is resurrected. And there will be thunder, lightning, earthquakes, breaking of solid rocks, tempests, collapsing mountains, empty cities, and even more potholes in the roads. Graves will open and the dead will rise; you'll even see saints appearing.

Now all this is true because an angel told it to Samuel. The only way to save yourself from eternal damnation is to repent and believe. This shouldn't be news to you people; something tells me you've heard it before a couple thousand times.

Just to be clear, Samuel reminds everyone that God used to love the Nephites and hate the Lamanites, but now it's all ass backwards. So repent already.

Many Nephites believe Samuel and go running to Nephi to confess their sins and be baptized.

Many others don't believe and start to stone the prophet Samuel! Behold, the stones can't hit him. So the nonbelievers shoot arrows, and these are redirected by the Lord. This miraculous force-field display changes even more Nephites into believers. But sadly, the vast majority remain wicked.

Samuel ends up fleeing back to the Lamanites and disappears.

For the next four years, angels appear to the Nephites trying to convince them of Christ's coming. The visits are met with skepticism and disbelief. The prevailing arguments are: Why would Jesus go to Jerusalem and not come here to see us on this continent? How are we supposed to believe unless

100 • C. B. BROOKS, M.D.

we see him? If he's God he can easily show up here too, right?

Satan also stirs such questions and thoughts among the Nephites. It's now the year 1 BC and the Book of Helaman ends.

16

Third Book of Nephi

If you recall, the Book of Mormon started off with the first and second Books of Nephi, narrated by Lehi's religious son named Nephi, who didn't get along with his brothers. Well, this Book of Nephi concerns a different Nephi, the son of Helaman, who was of course the son of Helaman, who was the son of Alma, who naturally was the son of Alma, who was a descendant of the original Nephi. For a person who obviously has no problem making up names, Joseph Smith seems to reuse a bunch. Anyway, this Book of Nephi has thirty chapters. We'd better get going.

This book's Nephi leaves the land of Zarahemla without a forwarding address and no one knows where the hell he went. He gives custody of the plates and sacred accessories to his son, who is named, you're not going to believe this, Nephi! (Couldn't he have named him Ralph or Jimmy?)

It's now 1 AD, and six hundred years since Lehi sailed from Jerusalem to the new continent. Lately, nothing much has happened and the people are starting to say that the prophecies of Samuel were a crock of goat droppings. The younger Nephi is our narrator and starts moaning about the lack of action, when the voice of God chimes in, "Hey, cheer up. Tomorrow's the day I arrive on Earth." And sure enough, at sunset it doesn't get dark, and at the next sunset a new bright star appears. Samuel's sign is really happening. Many convert and Nephi baptizes them.

Satan and the Gadianton robbers tell everyone, "It's just a coincidence, maybe a comet, or alien spacecraft," and they manage to maintain their large following of nonbelievers among the younger generations of Nephites and Lamanites.

Years pass and the memory of the miraculous signs start to fade. Wickedness seeps back in. The Gadianton robbers increase their numbers, commit murders, and sack numerous cities. Many Lamanites join the believing Nephites to resist the robbers. Civil war ensues.

Here's a shocker casually snuck into a verse—the Lamanites that united with the Nephites to fight the robbers actually turn white(!), and their offspring become white too (maybe even whiter!), so they are now called Nephites.

3 Nephi 2

13 And it came to pass that before this thirteenth year had passed away the Nephites were threatened with utter destruction because of this war, which had become exceedingly sore.

14 And it came to pass that those Lamanites who had united with the Nephites were numbered among the Nephites;

15 And their curse was taken from them, and their skin became white like unto the Nephites;

16 And their young men and their daughters became exceedingly fair, and they were numbered among the Nephites, and were called Nephites. And thus ended the thirteenth year.

More War

In 16 AD, Chief Judge Lachoneus receives a letter from the new leader of the Gadianton robbers, Giddianhi. (Alleluia, new names make a rebound.) The robber leader announces that he is the governor of the Secret Society of Gadianton, so please don't call us robbers anymore, we've gone mainstream. Giddianhi blows some smoke up Lachoneus's tunic', saying what a noble leader of the Nephites he is, then gets to the point: "Surrender up all your people, possessions, lands, and we can all be brethren. Otherwise, one month from now, my Secret Society army of robbers will descend from the wilderness and slay you. Discuss among yourselves and let me know." Your pal, Giddianhi.

Yikes.

Lachoneus comes up with a defensive plan. He appoints his man, Gidgiddoni (boo, hiss—too similar a name to the robber leader), as army captain. They urge all Nephites to gather their wives, animals, personal effects, and seven years' worth of provisions in the center of Zarahemla. Then they station guards and the army around the perimeter.

Having not received a reply to his friendly correspondence, Giddianhi and the robbers of Gadianton charge out of the wilderness, mountains, and secret hideouts. They easily conquer the abandoned lands and cities, but alas, there's no food or supplies to plunder, and the robbers (I mean Secret Society) have worked up an appetite. Giddianhi has no choice but to attack the Nephite defensive cluster in the heartland's center.

To scare the Nephites, the robbers wear lambskin loincloths and paint their entire bodies with blood, except for their head plates. They look like ferocious Native American braves from a John Wayne movie during their mass charge! The Nephites scream and fall to the ground. But it is only a fake collapse! The Nephites jump back up and engage in the bloodiest battle since Lehi landed in the new world. The Nephites prevail, and their Captain Gidgiddoni orders his troops to chase and slay as many painted robbers as they can catch. The robber leader, Giddianhi, is killed. The surviving robbers of Gadianton run back into the wilderness, where they stay for two years.

The Secret Society of robbers slowly reconstitutes an army under General Zemnarihah. They sally forth and surround the Nephite central settlement, attempting to starve them out. This fails because remember, the Nephites have brilliantly stockpiled seven years' worth of food. The robbers of Gadianton retreat from the siege and march toward the northern lands in search of food for themselves.

Nephite Captain Gidgiddoni makes a stealth, nighttime march cutting off their exit. He surprises the robber army, slaughters many, and takes the rest prisoner. Zemnarihah is hanged by the neck from a tree, and after he dies the tree is knocked down. Snap, take that.

The Nephites thank God with prayers and songs and become true believers once again. The captured robbers are put in prison, repent, and are converted.

Weird Interruption

For no apparent reason, in mid-chapter, Mormon butts in as narrator, saying that what you've been hearing is from the abbreviated plates. But he, Mormon, is making a record on his own plates with his own hands. Some babbling about history and covenants occurs. Okay readers, carry on.

Back to the Nephites

It is now safe for the Nephites to leave the central fort and go back to their homes in 26 AD. Prosperity and wealth returns, cities and roads are built.

Things progress well, but after a few years, wealth leads to pride, boastfulness, lawyers, merchants, income inequality, and loss of religion.

The church declines, gradually at first, and then almost disappears except for a few Lamanite faithful. Satan's influence grows.

Some prophets speak out against wickedness, but the local judges and lawyers have them quietly murdered, which is clearly illegal. They also secretly plot against the Chief Judge and want to have a king and noble class reinstituted.

In 30 AD, the Chief Judge is murdered, but the idea of anointing a king fails. Instead, the population breaks up into small tribes, each appointing a chief. Laws start to disintegrate.

Six years later, a secret cabal appoints one of its own chiefs as King Jacob. The other tribes rebel, and King Jacob and his people bug out to the far northern lands where they can start a kingdom.

Nephi is backing up his preaching by also performing miracles and casting out devils. He even brings his brother, a fellow prophet who was stoned to death, back to life! A few guys repent, but it's a losing battle. Nephi ordains priests and gives them the power to baptize converts (not that there were many).

A Big Sign
Just after 33 AD, the entire world turned dark for three full days—just like Samuel the Lamanite had prophesied! For three hours, the whole earth shook with the thunder and lightning of a huge category 5 tempest. The city of Zarahemla burned to the ground. The city of Moroni was swallowed by the angry sea and everyone drowned. A mountain clobbered the city of Moronihah. Southern and northern lands were destroyed. Earthquakes, whirlwinds, and fire destroyed more cities. Boulders were rent in two and cracks appeared in the ground.

The cataclysm died down but total darkness lasted three days. The only sounds were survivors moaning and lamenting that they should have repented.

A Loud Message
A voice is broadcast over the entire planet. It's Jesus Christ, the son of God, giving a long speech. Woe unto all who don't repent. This all happened because of your abominations and generally bad behavior. Jesus claims responsibility for destroying all the Nephite and Lamanite cities and mentions many of them, including the great city of Jacobugath, which was recently built by King Jacob and his tribe that moved north. You survivors, who are receiving this message, were spared because you're a little better then those just smitten, but not much. Don't get me wrong, I'm a merciful God, so

will you now receive me? Remember, it's the only way you can have eternal life, because I am all that, the Alpha and Omega, the light of the world. Don't bother anymore with your lame sacrifices and burnt offerings. You've really got to repent and be baptized. I laid down my life for you people.

The earth is completely silent for hours.

The voice returns, reminding everyone that they're descendants of the house of Israel, and Jesus is like a mother chicken gathering her chicks (yes, this is really in there). So repent already.

The next day the sun rises as usual and the planet settles back to normal. The semirighteous have been spared. Scriptures have been fulfilled, including the brass plates Lehi brought all the way from Jerusalem around six hundred years earlier.

Jesus on the New Continent Scene
It's still 34 AD. A large crowd is milling around the temple in the land Bountiful, when they hear a soft but piercing voice. It's God who speaketh an old Bible quote: "Behold my beloved son, in whom I am well pleased—Hear him."

Wow, everyone looks up toward heaven and sees Jesus descending, wearing a white bathrobe. He lands right in the middle of the awestruck crowd. He introduces himself and explains how he just recently died for all of mankind's sins. The people drop to the deck in amazement. As proof, in case there are any Doubting Thomases out there, JC lets them probe the wounds on his side and extremities. The audience is convinced.

Jesus then calls forth Nephi and gives him the power

to baptize (again). Instructions and clarifications are given regarding repentance, baptism, and the Holy Trinity (three gods in one: Father, Son, Holy Ghost). Anyone who disagrees is working for the devil.

Further oration with lots of purloined Bible quotes follow, making it crystal clear that all who repent and are baptized are saved; all who don't are damned with fire.

Jesus chooses twelve men from the crowd as disciples and gives them the power to baptize. A few chapters later we learn their names: Nephi, Timothy (Nephi's brother, whom Nephi raised from the dead), Jonas (Timothy's son), Mathoni, Mathonihah, Kumen (spice?), Kumenonhi, Jeremiah, Shemnon, Jonas (again), Zedekiah, and Isaiah.

Joseph Smith then has Jesus repeat a whole bunch of highlights from the Bible, such as: the Beatitudes (Blessed are they who …), salt of the earth, candle under a bushel, thou shalt not kill, or commit adultery even in your heart, the earth is God's footstool, turn the other cheek, love your enemies, the Lord's prayer, etc.

This recycling of Bible verses goes on for a few chapters. Then Jesus clues the audience in to the concept that they are his sheep too; they were just separated from the main flock in ancient Israel and sent to a new continent—and there are other sheep around the world that he'll be visiting next. So write these things down since the people in Israel may not know about you, and spread the word to any Gentiles you happen to meet.

Jesus' speech is getting lofty and hard to understand (maybe for Joseph Smith's exhausted scribe too), and he can tell he's losing the crowd. So he tells them to go home and ponder his words, then come back tomorrow for more teaching. And just to show he cares, Jesus tells them that his bowels are filled with compassion and mercy. Seriously. Then Jesus offers to perform some healings, just like he did in Jerusalem. The healings work and win back the crowd's attention!

No one wants to go home now, so as an encore, Jesus has all the kids approach and kneel in a circle around him. Jesus kneels down, groans, and prays to God the father. (Maybe about that bowel issue?) What he said can't be written, but it is good, and joy fills the arena. Jesus weeps twice and has the kids stand and look skyward. The heavens open, angels descend, and fire encircles the children. Risky but mesmerizing!

Wait, Jesus isn't done. He tells everyone to have a seat and sends the twelve disciples out to buy some bread and wine. When they return with the supplies, Jesus then breaks the bread and blesses it. He gives some to the disciples, then to the whole crowd, and says that he'll ordain someone to do this ritual (communion) to remember Jesus' body. Then he does the same ritual for the wine and gives everyone a sip to remember his blood.

He warns everyone that only the worthy can be allowed to participate in this communion procedure. The disciples are ordered to enforce this and forbid anyone deemed unworthy from partaking. Even so, they can keep ministering to the unworthy.

Jesus warns everyone to watch out for Satan the devil and to continue repenting and praying. Then he says he has to get going. He touches the hands of each of the twelve disciples and whispers that they also have the power to give the Holy Ghost. Then a cloud envelops the area and the people lose sight of

Jesus. The disciples verify that he ascended back into heaven. The crowd of 2,500 believers goes home.

Act 2

Word spreads throughout the land that Jesus Christ was here and is coming back tomorrow. People travel all night and form a humongous throng of humanity.

Nephi and the disciples take the stage and repeat the whole entire performance from yesterday. Then the multitudes move down to the river and mass baptisms occur, including Nephi and the chosen twelve disciples. Heaven opens up, angels descend, rings of fire encircle people, and your headliner, Jesus, arrives again and speaketh to the crowd!

There's ministering, kneeling, standing, a ton of praying, and the brilliant white light of the Spirit illuminates the disciples as bright and white as Jesus! The prayers are so awesome they couldn't be written down. Jesus praises the audience saying something like, "You're much better than the Jews I just spent thirty-three years with over in Israel. I couldn't show them this stuff because their faith wasn't as strong as yours!"

Jesus then commands everyone to be quiet, stand up, and continue to pray silently. He miraculously pulls out some bread and wine, blesses it, and passes it around. It's explained that this was a miracle because the disciples didn't bring any bread and wine with them today. Shazam!

Now for a new important message: Jesus says that God the father has authorized him to bestow this whole continent to you as your inheritance! Yes, you are descendants of the house of Jacob and Israel, so you deserve it! You'll also spread the word, conquer unbelievers, and Jesus'll help you out. You are officially children of God's covenant with Abraham. One day you'll unite together all the scattered tribes of Israel! A lot of over-the-top crazy rhetoric follows for chapters and chapters and chapters.

3 Nephi 20

19 For I will make my people with whom the Father hath covenanted, yea, I will make thy horn iron, and I will make thy hoofs brass. And thou shalt beat in pieces many people; and I will consecrate their gain unto the Lord, and their substance unto the Lord of the whole earth. And behold, I am he who doeth it.

3 Nephi 20

41 And then shall a cry go forth: Depart ye, depart ye, go ye out from thence, touch not that which is unclean; go ye out of the midst of her; be ye clean that bear the vessels of the Lord.

Jesus then calls up Nephi and asks him to show the records he's been keeping. Nephi spreads them out and Jesus, a speed reader, looks them over and says, "Hey, wait a minute, I told my prophet Samuel the Lamanite to announce that when I'm glorified, many saints should rise from the dead and appear and preach. Didn't Samuel say that?" Nephi answers, "Yea verily, he sure did predict that. And the dead saints did in fact rise and minister to us. Yes, sirree." And Jesus pimps him some more, "Well, why don't I see it written and expounded upon in these records? Umm, why is that Nephi?"

Nephi replies with something lame like, "I guess I forgot." So Jesus commands him to put it in there, like right now. (Geez, it's hard to get good scribes.)

Jesus provides more material to add to the records. A future messenger will come and purify people before Jesus returns again to judge the world. Sorcerers, adulterers, and bad bosses, among others, will be cut off. (True.) If you follow the rules, you'll be a blessed nation. Otherwise the Judgment Day will be quite dreadful.

The narrator identifies himself as Mormon, then points out that Jesus recounted the history of the world from the beginning to the last days for the crowd. There's not room to print all that information now, but the plates of Nephi contain it all anyway. Joseph Smith wanted to include it (all over again!), but the Lord forbade him (or maybe the scribe threatened to resign).

Jesus continues to teach, perform healings, and raise the dead for three solid days. Then he ascends again to heaven, this time without any fanfare. The disciples go forth and baptize, and allegedly see things so miraculous that they can't be written because they're against the law! All the new folks baptized are called the Church of Christ (which coincidentally was the first name of Joseph Smith's church before it was called the Mormon Church or Church of Jesus Christ of Latter-day Saints).

Cameo Appearance

The disciples are on a road tour preaching. One day, when they are all together praying, who shows up again but Jesus! He gives them a pep talk and recycles another bunch of Bible references such as: ask and you'll receive, knock and it will open, etc. Then he asks if he can do anything for them? Yes, as a matter of fact, they want clarification on the name of the

Church of Christ, and Jesus verifies it.

Jesus then asks each disciple: "If you could have anything, what would it be?" Nine of the twelve ask to come to heaven when they die. Jesus says, "That's fine, I'll bring you up there when you all die at age seventy-two." (Oops, a little too much information. Possible first use of the term "Jesus Christ, TMI bro.")

The other three disciples remain silent. Jesus approaches and indicates that he's reading their minds and knows what they want: it's the same thing John supposedly wanted when Jesus was over in Jerusalem. Jesus grants their wish—they will be immortal!

Heaven opens up and the three are beamed up and changed into immortal beings. They still look sort of the same but they'll never die, or feel pain or sorrow, or be swayed by the devil.

The three return to earth and continue preaching across the world to Nephites, Gentiles, and Jews. They're thrown in prisons, furnaces, wild-beast cages, and deep pits, but nothing can hold or harm them! Whoa! Who are these three? Sorry, but the Lord forbade the narrator, Mormon, from revealing their identities. But rest assured it's true because he's seen them and they will continue to walk the earth until the great second coming when they'll join Jesus on Judgment Day.

Just to be crystal clear, more reminders about repenting follow.

Time out. Maybe Joseph Smith's scribe interrupts and asks a question, because the narrator abruptly shifts gears and says he has inquired of the Lord how these three disciples could possibly walk the earth forever, which would mean that they're currently among us and would be exceedingly old by now. And the Lord answers with the technical point that in order to avoid the taste of death, their bodies underwent a change; not the change like on Judgment Day, which is the really big change, but more like a sanctifying in the flesh sort of thing. (Sounds like some fancy footwork, but this is where the Mormon idea that Three Nephite Disciples, whose identities are secret, roam the Earth and even today work to save the faithful. As you can imagine, this has led to unofficial identifications, sightings, and rumored close encounters between believers and the clandestine trio.)

Two unusually short chapters end this book. All the prophecies will be fulfilled. No need to spurn the Lord. Gentiles start to repent.

17

Fourth Book of Nephi

I'm suspicious. Something must have happened between Joseph Smith and his scribe, or within Joseph Smith himself. First, the abrupt explanation and ending of the previous book is an unusual departure from the narrator's typical style we've come to know. Next, this Fourth Book of Nephi is really short, only one chapter; whereas the First, Second, and Third Books of Nephi were extremely long-winded. Plus, this one brief chapter covers almost three hundred years of history! The narrative crawled along through the years with excruciating detail, and now it's suddenly at warp speed? Maybe Joseph Smith lost his mojo, or burned out? Maybe his scribe threw a bull-pucky flag on the three immortal disciples who roam the earth, or the scribe freaked out about having to transcribe three hundred more years of repetitive history, or maybe he developed writer's cramp or carpal tunnel syndrome? In any case, you be the judge.

The years 34 and 35 AD come to an end. The disciples have successfully started the Church of Christ all around the continent. In 36 AD, every inhabitant, Nephite and Lamanite, is converted as a good church-going member. No arguments occur, incomes are equal, no rich or poor, freedom and peace reign.

Years pass in this utopia. The disciples perform miracles and healings, and raise the dead routinely. Cities are rebuilt, but some can't be salvaged because they are flooded or sunken into the earth. The Nephites multiply as a white and delightful race.

The nine mortal disciples die and go to heaven. The immortal three continue on, doing the Lord's work on Earth. New disciples are ordained.

Everything is perfect—no fights, whoredoms, lies, or crimes of any sort. No robbers, no Lamanites even—everyone is a child of God.

Nephi passes the plates to his son Amos around 84 AD. A small group leaves the church and calls themselves Lamanites.

Amos dies around 194 AD and gives the plates and Fourth Book of Nephi to his son, also named Amos.

It's 200 AD, and "I, Mormon" butts in again relating what happened for the next few hundred years. This is getting bizzarre. Mormon was telling us what went down around 30-something AD like he was an eyewitness in the Third Book of Nephi. How old is he anyway? (Standby, more confusion coming in the next chapter.)

In 201 AD, some folks start to be prideful, wear expensive clothes, and horde wealth. No more classless utopia around here. Rival churches spring up. Some of these churches provide the bread and wine communion to the unworthy—an act expressly forbidden by Jesus.

By 210 AD, Satan's back in business. One church denies Christ and bullies the official Church of Christ. The disciples are tossed into jail, but fortunately the prison is ripped into two halves, allowing them to escape and continue performing miracles.

People with hardened hearts and stiff necks again try hurling the disciples into furnaces and wild-beast cages, but they are unharmed.

Believers are persecuted, but they turn the other cheek and do not fight back.

In 231 AD the population is divided. True believers are called Nephites, a designation that includes the Jacobites, Josephites, and Zoramites. Those who reject Jesus are called Lamanites, Lemuelites, and Ishmaelites. They are wicked, abominable, and hate the Nephites, as you can imagine.

By 244 AD, the Lamanites are a large majority. The delightsome Nephites start to be prideful and rich, losing their faith. Gadianton robbers start reorganizing.

By 300 AD, both Nephites and Lamanites are thoroughly wicked. In 305, Amos dies and hands off the plates to his brother Ammaron (near name recycle).

In 320 AD, Ammaron "hides up all the plates and sacred records unto the Lord, so they might come again to the chosen people, someday in the future." This is how it's described—no further details are given.

The short book ends. This is a major shift in writing style and recording. The years and events have been briefly listed in starkly abbreviated terms in this Fourth Book of Nephi.

18

Book of Mormon

This is the title of the next book, which comprises only nine chapters. It has the same title as the overall work, the Book of Mormon.

Mormon is the narrator and continues the historical record. Mormon initially describes himself as being a very precocious (and sober) ten-year-old! Ammaron, after hiding all the plates, goes to visit the young lad Mormon and gives him an assignment for the future. When Mormon becomes twenty-four, he should go to a hill called Shim in the land of Antum and find the sacred plates. He should then take the plates of Nephi and engrave the history he observes on them and leave all the other plates on Shim.

Hold it. Official time-out. How long has Mormon been around? I seem to recall him interrupting other books for literally centuries. How can Mormon be a ten-year-old rascal now in the early 300 ADs? A quick clarification about Mormon's age is served up via parentheses:

Mormon 1

5 And I, Mormon, being a descendant of Nephi, (and my father's name was Mormon) I remembered the things which Ammaron commanded me.

Could this be in response to an objection by Joseph's scribe, who might be questioning the chronology—just like I am? Oh, well, it's simple really. Perhaps this isn't the same Mormon—it's his son, also named Mormon, so that should resolve any perceived timeline irregularities, which by the way are present in the sacred texts of just about every religion. Or maybe Mormon was just altering the older plates with comments in the margins, okay? Now can we please continue with our divinely inspired story, you surly scribe? Thank you.

Where was I? When Mormon is a young teen, he mentions a battle between the Nephites and their associated tribes and the Lamanites and their associated tribes. Then peace occurs, but wickedness is rampant over all the lands. The Lord is disappointed and recalls his ambassadors, the disciples, from performing healings and miracles. The Holy Ghost leaves town too.

Mormon turns fifteen and is visited by the Lord. Mormon is eager to preach but God muzzles him.

The Gadianton robbers infiltrate all areas. The people hide their treasure by burying it in the ground (good news for future gold and treasure diggers like Joseph Smith).

A war breaks out in 326 AD. Fifteen-year-old Mormon, who was physically large, is appointed General of the Nephite armies. Very sparse details are given. There's another war the next year against the huge Lamanite army. The Nephite military is frightened and runs away to the city of Angola and fortifies it. The Lamanites attack and drive them out.

The Nephite army gets chased through numerous lands. They try to rally the people but there's no will to fight because they're infested with Lamanites and robbers of Gadianton.

Mormon briefly explains that he did defeat the larger Lamanite force under the command of King Aaron.

The Nephites, instead of repenting and getting right with Jesus, openly curse God instead!

The Lamanite army returns and the Nephite people run to the northern city of Jashon, which coincidentally was near the hill where Ammaron had hidden the plates.

Mormon leads the Nephites against a larger Lamanite force and wins, but the people's hearts just aren't in it. Some lands are reclaimed. In 350 AD a treaty is negotiated, giving the Lamanites and robbers all the southern lands.

Ten years pass. God visits Mormon and tells him to try to get the Nephites to repent, but they just won't do it. Their hearts are hardened.

The Nephites are clustered in the land of Desolation. For two years the Lamanites attack and are repelled. Instead of turning to God, the Nephites boast about their victories.

Mormon is so ticked off he resigns as general of the army. He complains to God, who replies that the Nephites will see his godly vengeance someday.

In 363, the Nephites are emboldened and attack the Lamanites. The Lamanite army drives them back and out of Desolation. The Nephites retreat to the city of Teancum.

The next year Lamanites attack and are repulsed. Nephites regain Desolation and brag about it.

The year 366 brings a bloody battle and both sides are so wicked they actually enjoy the slaughter! The Lamanites take Desolation and Teancum and capture Nephite women and children. The filthy Lamanites sacrifice the prisoners to their false-idol gods.

The Nephites are so mad, they attack again the next year and retake the cities.

In 375 the Lamanites counterattack with an overwhelming force. Nephites are driven back into the city of Boaz. More women and children prisoners are turned into human sacrifices. The Lamanites are on the verge of conquering the entire land.

Things look so bad that Mormon goes up to the hill Shim and collects all the plates. (Looks like he missed his appointment to do this when he was twenty-four. But why quibble—the whole continent is going to hell in a hurry.) Then he takes command of the Nephite army again, but knows it's a lost cause. The Nephites are despairing but still won't repent.

Multiple Lamanite attacks are rebuffed, but all smaller towns and villages are burned to the ground. In 380 a huge Lamanite army descends and the Nephites flee. Many are chased down and killed.

The Final Battle
Mormon explains to us that he'll write down the events as he was commanded, but emphasizes that there's a ton of wickedness goin' down.

Mormon leads the Nephite army out to face the Lamanites. He sends an epistle letter to King Aaron inviting him to meet the Nephite army and people at the hill called Cumorah for a big battle. The King agrees to attend and will be delighted to bring his massive Lamanite army.

It's now 384 AD. The stage is set for an epic, final battle. The people of Nephi are gathered and camped in the land Cumorah. Mormon is getting old and knows this will be his last engagement. God has commanded him not to let the plates get captured, because the Lamanites will destroy them. So he hides most of the plates up in the hill Cumorah but continues to write on a few plates that he gives to his son Moroni.

An innumerable Lamanite army arrives at Cumorah. The fair-skinned Nephite people are filled with terror at the sight. The Lamanites attack and mow down the Nephites with arrows, axes, and swords. Tens upon tens of thousands of Nephites are slaughtered. Mormon is wounded. A group of twenty-four, including his son Moroni, survive. A few Nephites run away, and a few defect over to the Lamanites, but the people of Nephi are essentially destroyed. Bodies litter the landscape.

Mormon and the twenty-four survivors survey the battlefield and Mormon cries out, mourning how they should have repented.

Aftermath

Mormon addresses some remarks to the survivors, telling them that they can't be saved without repenting, and reminding them that they're a remnant of the house of Israel. He recounts how Jesus Christ was the son of God, was murdered by the Jews, and rose from the dead. There's going to be a Judgment Day sometime in the future when all the dead will be resurrected and either saved or damned.

So please repent and be baptized. This record will come from the Jews to the Gentiles and then to you, so you'll know what happened and how awesome God has been. Amen.

Moroni Time
Mormon's son Moroni now keeps the true records and narrates.

The Nephites who escaped southward from the mammoth battle were hunted down by the Lamanites and killed. Mormon was one of them! Moroni is all alone and hides the plates by burying them in the ground.

It's 400 AD and the Lamanites have completely exterminated the Nephites, except for Moroni. The Lamanites and robbers are all that remain. They're now fighting among themselves in constant bloodshed.

No one believes in God—except the disciples God abducted from the population—but no one knows where they went.

A Little Self-Promotion
Moroni praises the future person who is chosen to discover the plates (that's our boy Joseph Smith!). That person will be blessed by God for bringing this valuable information out of its hiding place deep in the earth, and shining it forth like a beacon of knowledge for the people, by the power of the Lord!

Oh, and if there are any mistakes in the record, just let them slide; they're just faults of man, not God. Only God punishes mistakes; it's not your role to criticize. Clerical or miscellaneous errors are perfectly acceptable. (Well that clears things up. Now I won't even ask if this is the same Moroni who scalped the Lamanite general back in the first century BC.

Maybe he was a distant cousin, or reincarnated, or there was just a transcription error.)

Joseph rocks on with the momentous news. Once these truths are revealed, the saints that dwelt in this land will cry to God and he'll renew his covenant.

These truths will be revealed in a future time when many bad churches, full of proud and money-grubbing preachers, are present throughout the land. (Like the contemporary time of Joseph Smith perhaps?)

For the Nonbelievers
Moroni then launches into a fiery speech exhorting the nonbelievers. He warns them that you can't wait until Judgment Day to see Christ and then suddenly believe. It's just too late then, my brothers.

There used to be great miracles back when people believed, but we don't have them anymore because of unbelief. So, harken up you people. Earthly life is a probation test, and you're all failing it. Repent, clean up your acts, yak yak yak.

Housekeeping Note
Before ending, Moroni points out that he and Mormon wrote these plates in reformed Egyptian font, because it's nice and small. So there might be some mistakes. If the plates had been bigger, they would've used Hebrew, and then, of course, they would've been perfect. Just saying. So stop being picky.

Mormon 9

32 And now, behold, we have written this record according to our knowledge, in the characters which are called among us the reformed Egyptian, being handed down and altered by us, according to our manner of speech.

33 And if our plates had been sufficiently large we should have written in Hebrew; but the Hebrew hath been altered by us also; and if we could have written in Hebrew, behold, ye would have had no imperfection in our record.

19

Book of Ether

Moroni continues as narrator of this fifteen-chapter book. Remember, he is the sole remaining survivor of the Nephite people, so he probably needed something to do. Here's a project: why not tell the tale of that mysterious civilization that got wiped out in the north country? Splendid idea.

Moroni explains that he's taking this from the twenty-four plates that were found by the people of Limhi. These plates contain the Book of Ether, originally written by a prophet named Ether. The plates tell a two-part story. Part one starts with the creation of the universe, Adam and Eve, the history of the Jews, and the Tower of Babel. Moroni graciously spares us the repetitive part one and focuses on part two, which takes us from the time of the tower until the time these north-country folks are obliterated.

Okay, let's roll. Moroni starts with a long family tree that ends with Ether, who was a son of Corianton, who was a son of Moron (not Mormon, but Moron). I kid you not, there is actually a character named Moron. I guess the term hadn't yet derived its modern meaning back in 1830? Either that or Joseph Smith was making a not-so-subtle point?

The genealogy continues backward in time. Some names are repeats, some are biblical, but Joseph Smith still has some firepower left with names like: Ahah, Com, Amnigaddah, Hearthom, Kib, Lib, Riplakish, Shez, and many more. Finally, after nearly thirty generations, this genealogical list reaches Jared. (Not to be confused with the convicted pedophile Jared formerly of Subway.)

Anywho, Jared lived at the time of the Tower of Babel. (It's not discussed here, but for those who don't know, the Old Testament Bible has a story about humans getting upitty and building a tower to try to reach heaven. Yahweh, the Jewish God, is insulted by the project, so he scatters the people and gives them different languages so they can't communicate with each other and come up with a stupid idea like this again. Hence the tower was named Babel, as in babble.) Jared knew God was mad about the tower construction, so he asked his brother to approach God and beseech him not to scatter his family or confound their tongues. They also requested that if they do get scattered, that the family get sent to a really nice place.

God has pity on Jared's group and says to gather the extended family, friends, animals, and possessions and meet him in the valley of Nimrod.

They meet up and God tells them to start building barges, for they'll all be sailing to a wonderful destination, described as prime real estate, and will form a great nation. There's only one condition: when they arrive, they must serve God, or they will be swept off the face of the earth. Sounds fair enough.

God leads them through the wilderness and has them camp by the seashore for four years. God finally returns and gives more instructions on barge building. There should be eight barges, watertight, covered on top, no windows, and have a corked hole in the top and the bottom. When the brothers question this design, God appears to them in the form of Jesus Christ, who by the way hasn't arrived on Earth yet.

Jesus explains that he is the son of God the father but they're still one God. He actually shows Jared's brother the answers to all the mysteries of the world and shows what will happen in the future! (Yo, JC, I was just asking about the corks!) Jesus Christ tells him to write all these things down on plates but keep them secret. "Use a secret language no one can read." Jesus touches sixteen stones with his finger and they turn transparent like glass. Two of these become the magical seer stones that will allow the plates to be deciphered. "Keep the stones with the plates and seal them up."

Wow! These were the plates with the secret information—not to be shared with humans, until after Jesus Christ is crucified—that were alluded to by King Mosiah. And the seer stones too!

Moroni continues this tangent storyline for a few chapters. In the present tense, he explains that he has the plates and that Jesus has indeed been crucified already, but that there aren't any believers left to share them with—only lousy nonbelieving Lamanites. So Moroni must write his additions on the plates, then seal them up with the two seer interpreter stones. They won't be revealed to the Gentiles until a point in the future, when there exist faithful, trustworthy guardians to reveal them to. There will be three witnesses chosen to help reveal the plates and testify to their authenticity. And anyone who won't believe or who argues will be cursed. When these plates are revealed, you'll know God's work has commenced. Whoa! This is a Joseph Smith Jr. self-advertisement and a revelation of his plan to give three lucky witnesses an opportunity for fame and holiness. (Something tells me this was to keep the scribes interested. We've already had hints of their restlessness.)

Back to the Barges
One complaint the brothers raise to God about the barge design is that they are fully enclosed and very dark inside. God explains that they're enclosed because the barges will be submerging under huge waves in a massive flood he's going to be sending. Yes, they are indeed dark, but remember those stones Jesus touched with his finger? Well, eight of them will glow and serve as lights. Problem solved.

Now get on board everyone, and don't forget to bring food. God sends a wind to shove off the barges toward the promised land. A huge tempest roars in with tsunami-size waves. The barges are alternately buried under water, then tossed high onto wave crests. The illuminating stones work well providing light. No mention of seasickness is made.

The barges finally hit land and the passengers praise God. Everyone starts farming and making babies.

Jared and his brother grow old and wish to retire. The people decide they want a king. All the sons of the brothers refuse, except one, who is crowned King Orihah. Jared and his unnamed brother, who knew the answers to all the mysteries of the world but apparently didn't share, die.

Royal Treatment

King Orihah actually performs well. His son succeeds him, King Kib. Kib rules from the land of Moron. Kib's son, Corihor, rebels and starts a breakaway settlement in the land of Nehor.

Corihor attracts a following and builds up an army. The army marches to Moron and takes his father, King Kib, captive. Corihor now rules.

Another soap opera develops, but luckily in shorthand form. Briefly, imprisoned King Kib's youngest son, Shule, is angry at older brother Corihor. Shule makes swords, raises an army, and rescues King Kib. Kib is grateful and makes Shule the new King. Corihor says he's sorry. Corihor's son Noah challenges King Shule and wins a battle, taking King Shule prisoner and transporting him back to Moron land. Noah's about to execute King Shule, when Schule's sons burst in, kill Noah, and rescue dad. The son of Noah, named Cohor, continues Noah's renegade kingdom. King Shule reigns again in his kingdom.

These two kingdoms then go to war. Shule wins, Cohor is slain. Cohor's son Nimrod surrenders the outlaw kingdom to King Shule and is rewarded.

Prophets start to appear, warning of idolatry and urging repentance. King Shule backs them up and things go well.

More Lunacy

This fast-motion story races ahead at breakneck speed. King Omer succeeds Shule. Omer has a shifty son, Jared, who has a shifty daughter. Jared rebels, battles his father King Omer, and jails him for years. Omer's other sons enlist an army and wage a nighttime battle, defeating Jared. Jared says he'll return the kingdom to Omer if they spare his life. They agree and King Omer is reinstated.

Jared's beautiful but cunning daughter concocts a plot with Jared. They'll invite a big dude, Akish, over for dinner. The daughter will perform a pole dance for him and he'll desire her for his wife. Jared will agree as long as Akish vows to bring King Omer's head to him on a nice plate. (Extremely reminiscent of the New Testament Bible story of John the Baptist's demise.)

The plan is set in motion. Akish falls for it but he's cunning too. He marries the crafty daughter. God warns King Omer, who leaves town. Akish has his own plan and swears his loyal henchmen to secrecy. Since King Omer fled, his son Jared is now king, and Akish is his new son-in-law. Without delay, Akish has his men lop off King Jared's head while he sits on his fancy new throne. Akish is now king by default.

Moroni chimes in that secret societies and secret oaths are the work of Satan and never end well.

King Akish's sons bribe the people to rise up against their dad. Civil war ensues for years and decimates the population down to only thirty people!

King Omer returns from exile and retakes the throne. His son Emer follows. Omer dies after a sad life. God throws King Emer a bone and sixty-two years of prosperity follow. Riches flow, and exotic animals like elephants, cumons, and cureloms are used to assist man here on our continent. (Cumons and cureloms are two make-believe animals found nowhere on Earth except in the Book of Mormon! No description is given.) King Emer's son Coriantum takes over and builds cities. King Coriantum's childless wife dies at age 102, so he marries a young chambermaid who bears children. Coriantum dies happy at age 142.

A succession of kings follows. The people spread across the land. Oops, wickedness returns. Heth dethrones and kills his father King Com (not King Kong). Prophets reappear and predict a curse, but the people ignore the dire warnings. The prophets are tossed into pits to die.

Drought and dearth appear throughout the land. People, including King Heth, die of starvation. Poisonous snakes show up and bite humans and livestock. Survivors migrate and eat animal carcasses killed by the poisonous snakes.

God throttles the agony down a bit, and fruit starts to grow in the north country. King Shez rebuilds things. His son, King Riplakish, is bad news. He takes many wives and concubines, taxes the people, starts debtor prisons, amasses riches, and has prisoners make jewelry for him. Forty-two years of whoredom follow, until the population revolts and kills King Riplakish.

Years later, one of his descendants, Morianton, battles back and becomes king. The people like him, but God cuts him off because of excessive "whoring around." (Yes, that happened.)

More and more of the same—kings taken prisoner by sons, over and over. (I'll spare you the boring details.) Prosperity returns until the kingdom splits between Com and Amgid. Com wins and reunites the land, but robbers start to form secret groups and plot treachery.

Prophets again predict doom unless everyone repents. Com's son, King Shiblon, takes over and his brother rebels and wants to kill all the prophets. (Because, face it, they're annoying.) They counter with even more visions of destruction and heaps of bones on the land.

Wars, king slayings, rebellions, and more generations of royalty follow. Prophets proliferate under evil King Ethem and predict utter devastation. The people won't listen, so the prophets leave town, temporarily. Ethem's son, King Moron(!), is even worse.

King Moron is overthrown and jailed. While in captivity, he fathers Coriantor, who spends his entire life in prison! Somehow the imprisoned Coriantor fathers Ether, who becomes a prophet.

Under the new King Coriantumr, Ether becomes an unstoppable prophet because he has the Spirit of God. He cries out from sunrise to past sunset, exhorting everyone to repent and embrace God, or else guess what, ye be destroyed.

Disclaimer

Moroni can't help but interject an editorial comment about how faith is actually an invisible thing, so don't question it, okay. Faith makes everything possible, including everything in this book, and he lists some highlights.

He predicts some may mock these things, but that's just due to our human weak writing ability, because our hands are so awkward. (Something tells me the scribe couldn't take it anymore.)

God then speaketh to Moroni, saying only fools mock, but they'll be sorry. (Possible nasty look toward scribe?) Faith is where it's at, and did I mention it's invisible? There's no hope without faith.

Moroni signs off, apologizing for the short interruption, and blaming it on his weak writing skills.

Give Us Some Ether Please

Ether predicts a new Jerusalem coming down from heaven onto this new continent. It will be of the house of Joseph from Egypt. The blood of the lamb, our redeemer, will sanctify it. All those scattered tribes will come together here. More Bible quotes are copied and pasted into his speech too.

Sorry, but the population just isn't buying Ether's message, so they chuck him out of the city. Ether lives in a "cavity of a rock" by day and comes out at night to record the events.

That year, a great war starts between the robbers and King Coriantumr. None of the light-skinned people repent. Many die in the war.

The next year, God sends Ether back to give Coriantumr another chance to repent and save his people. To sweeten the offer, Ether also tells King Coriantumr that God won't let him be slain by the sword if he accepts. Sorry, no deal. The King tries to slay Ether, but Ether narrowly escapes back to his rock cavity.

King Coriantumr is overthrown and taken captive by Shared. The sons of Coriantumr restore their dad to the throne four years later. Coriantumr musters armies against Shared for revenge.

War spreads across the continent again, this time even between neighborhoods. It's a free-for-all. Robbers roam the land. Coriantumr chases down Shared and wins. Then Shared beats back Coriantumr and wins. Then Coriantumr beats Shared again and kills him. But during the struggle, Shared wounds Coriantumr in the leg and it takes him two years to recover. War continues between anyone who can fight.

Another curse falls on the continent: if you happen to put

your sword down, even for a second, it disappears! So everyone keeps their swords on them at all times. It is an armed society with everyone defending their houses.

Shared's brother shows up with an army and fights Coriantumr's troops, who are defeated at night because they're completely drunk. Shared's bro, Gilead, takes the throne.

Coriantumr rebuilds his army for two years in the wilderness while his leg heals.

Gilead's high priest murders him as he sits on the throne. Lib, the biggest dude in the land, takes over.

Coriantumr enters the land of Moron and fights Lib. They chase each other and battle all over the region. Lib is killed. His brother, Shiz (oh, another unfortunate adolescence most likely), leads the army against Coriantumr, who runs away on his rehabilitated leg. Shiz chases him and conquers many cities.

Shiz rolls up territory and gains recruits. The rest of the populace joins Coriantumr's army. All-out war rages so much that the entire continent is covered in bodies. Worms eat them. A bad stench develops.

Shiz pins Coriantumr's army up against the sea. More battles occur. Shiz smites Coriantumr and almost kills him. (Which would invalidate Ether's prophecy.) Luckily, Coriantumr recovers, again.

Two million of Coriantumr's people have now died, and he starts to have second thoughts about all this warfare. So he writes an epistle proposing peace to Shiz: Dear Shiz-head. Oops, that was a bad start. Surprisingly, Shiz is open to the idea of peace. He writes back saying he'll spare all Coriantumr's people, but he wants to skewer Coriantumr personally with a sword. Huh, well this would violate Ether's prophecy, so Coriantumr declines the deal. By the way, no repenting is going on anywhere.

Battles resume. Retreats, chases, skirmishes, and lots of camping follow. Coriantumr gets slashed again, and faints from blood loss, but recovers. More fighting.

The Grand Finale
Finally, four years later, the entire population joins either Coriantumr's or Shiz's army. I mean every person: men, women, and children; no one is on the sidelines. Everyone has a weapon, even the babies.

Full-on, cage-match, no-holds-barred warfare occurs every day, followed by nighttime relaxation. Each night the survivors let out a bone-chilling howl that sweeps the land.

Coriantumr tries another letter to Shiz, hopefully more diplomatic this time. There's no Spirit of the Lord around anymore. Both armies hate each other and want to fight. So the daily carnage continues.

Eventually the sides are slaughtered down to Coriantumr's fifty-four fighters and Shiz's sixty-nine fighters. The next day, thirty-two Shiz fighters remain versus twenty-seven Coriantumr fighters. Three hours of nonstop sword fighting mows down even more.

On the third day each side is whittled down to an army of one: King Coriantumr against the mighty Shiz himself. A mano-a-mano, winner-take-all, fight-to-the-death grudge match.

Swordplay, fisticuffs, and back-and-forth hair-pulling drama follow until Shiz passes out from loss of blood!

Coriantumr staggers over, rests a second, and lops off the head of Shiz. But Shiz isn't done! Even without his head, he rears up on his hands, gasps, and dramatically dies. Coriantumr drops to the ground and looks dead too. There's only one person left, our prophet Ether.

God tells Ether to check the situation out and finish writing his plates. Ether agrees and hides the twenty-four plates somewhere the future people of Limhi can find them.

Authors note: That's how the Book of Ether ends. Not really explaining what happened to Coriantumr or Ether. Maybe a setup for a sequel?

The modern Church of Jesus Christ of Latter-day Saints calls the people of this story the Jaredites, after Jared who led them across the ocean in the barges. But the term Jaredite never appears in the actual text.

20

Book of Moroni

This is the last book within the Book of Mormon. It has ten short chapters. Moroni is our narrator.

He starts off explaining how he's finished writing his history of the people of Jared. He's also hiding from the Lamanites, in fear for his life.

The Lamanites are savagely fighting among themselves. They're also killing any Nephite they find who refuses to deny belief in Jesus Christ. Moroni certainly won't deny Christ, so he's in danger and knows it. Nevertheless, Moroni says he will write some extra information on the plates, so Lamanites might use it someday if it's ever revealed to them (maybe by a holy prophet like Joseph Smith?). Indeed, it looks like Joseph Smith is using this section to clarify and establish some doctrines and rituals he's planning on using in his church.

Remember those twelve disciples Jesus Christ personally anointed? Well, Moroni tells us that if one of them lays their hands on you, you shall receive the Holy Ghost. And once you have it, you can give it to others. In case anyone questions this power, Jesus himself secretly said it to the disciples when he visited the continent.

The disciples are the first elders of the church. The power of the Holy Ghost that they confer is what makes it possible for them to ordain priests and teachers, and to forgive sins.

Moroni then explains the procedure for distributing the body (bread) and blood (wine) of Christ.

We also learn that three witnesses have the power to condemn sinners before the elders and get them kicked out of the church unless they repent.

Baptism you ask? Well, here it is. It's for those who repent. Once baptized, they become members of the church.

Moroni shifts gears and adds some sayings of his deceased father, Mormon. An evil man can't do good. All good comes from God. Evil comes from the devil. You really need faith, hope, and charity. Pray. Repent. Everything I've said is true. A lot of verses follow, but nothing new.

Next, Moroni talks about a letter Mormon wrote to him settling some things that have caused disputes. I'm talking about baptism of children. It's an abomination, a big error, a mockery, so get rid of it fast! Little kids can't sin, so they don't need baptism. Little kids can't repent either. Baptism's for adults who've sinned and repented. Anyone who disagrees should be condemned and cast out, and they'll also get some eternal torment!

Now for another letter from Mormon to Moroni. Mormon is with the Nephites fighting against the Lamanites and receives unsettling news from Amoron. "The Lamanites have taken prisoners and forced them to eat each other—cannibalism! The Nephites aren't much better. They won't repent and have taken Lamanite women prisoners and stolen their chastity, then tortured and murdered them, then ate them for dinner." Mormon is distraught, "Oh man! And Nephites used to be delightful. This is so outrageous, God's got to deliver some holy judgment, and soon. We're surrounded by depraved Lamanites, but our Nephites are worse if you can believe that! Things are so bad it can't even be written. If I mention God or repentance around here, they'll smite me! Keep the faith, Moroni! Hope to see you soon." Your dad, Mormon.

Moroni finishes up the final chapter in 421 AD by writing a message for the surviving Lamanites in case they ever find these plates. The Nephites have been wiped out. Moroni exhorts the Lamanites to remember how merciful the Lord has been. So don't deny Christ, or God, or the Holy Ghost. Realize that God gives many gifts, and Moroni names a bunch. Then he offers a repeat summary on faith, hope, and charity. Unbelief will cause a world of trouble, and of course you won't be saved. The time's coming soon and you'll find out I'm not lying, because you'll see me, Moroni, standing at the "bar of the Lord," and you'll be damned. Better get perfect with Christ.

Moroni bids a quick farewell. He's going to rest in God's paradise, until his body and soul are reunited through the air at the Great Judgment. The end.

Section III

MORMONISM: AN ANALYSIS

That wraps up Joseph Smith Jr.'s Book of Mormon—an alternate history that starts around 600 years before Christ in the vicinity of Jerusalem and ends about 421 AD on a different continent. A rambling history purportedly engraved on metal plates in a foreign language. A secret history trove that lay dormant until Joseph Smith Jr. dug up the plates himself using divine directions received through visions in the early 1800s.

Wow.

Lucky for us that Moroni appeared to Joseph Smith and inspired him to not only translate the secret plates but also to have the transcript published. Otherwise we'd never have known all this incredible religious, political, cultural, social, geographical, racial, and military history. We'd never have known that Jesus visited our hemisphere after he was crucified and allegedly rose from the dead over in the Middle East. And we'd never have had the basis for a uniquely American religion, the Church of Jesus Christ of Latter-day Saints, commonly called Mormonism. Now you know what the Mormons believe as facts. Consider for a moment we almost had our first Mormon president of the United States in 2012, Republican candidate Mitt Romney.

After reading the tedious, repetitive, long, and disjointed Book of Mormon from cover to cover, and passing on a hopefully more entertaining synopsis to you, I'm stunned at how anyone could believe this. Likewise, after reading the Bible from cover to cover for my book *The Nonbeliever's Guide to Bible Stories*, I was shocked anyone could believe what's contained in the Bible too. In fact, most all world religions unquestioningly rely on holy books of scripture as their foundation. In my experience, when you actually read and examine them, they're completely without evidence and rather ridiculous.

As I wrote in my first book, *Trust Your Radar, Honest Advice for Teens and Young Adults from a Surgeon, Firefighter, Police Officer, Scuba Divemaster, Golfer, and Amateur Comedian*, religion is a potent jammer of our human brain radars. We explore why religions appeal to our primitive brain circuits, and how it takes courage to challenge accepted tenets of faith. Ultimately, all religions rely on the concept of faith for people to suspend reasonable thinking and accept the unbelievable without evidence. As Peter Boghossian, author of *A Manual for Creating Atheists*, explains: "Faith is pretending to know what you really don't." Certainly seems to apply here—at least for those who came to adopt, follow, and advance the religion. But what about Joseph Smith Jr.? What explains him?

21

Joseph Smith Jr.: Prophet, Fraud, or Something Else?

Even though Joseph Smith Jr. assigns various characters as narrators of the chapters, he was actually the sole narrator of the Book of Mormon—it was all him. Although he claimed to have been translating his words from secret metal plates—that no other human actually saw with their own eyes—the elaborate histories, crazy names, and soaring religious orations are all the products of his mind, dictated to rapidly scribbling scribes. Further, he lifted choice verses straight from the Bible.

My main question throughout this project has been: What made Joseph Smith Jr. tick? What drove this man?

It seems to me that there are three possible explanations, the last being my personal conclusion. The first possibility is that Joseph actually was visited by God and Moroni. He truly dug up the sacred plates, hid them from others as instructed, used two seer stones as magical glasses to translate the engravings, dictated the Book of Mormon by divine inspiration, and handed the physical plates back to God. He then started his church, met external resistance, faced dissension within the church, and died a martyr and great American prophet. Members of the Church of Jesus Christ of Latter-day Saints would ascribe to this view.

The second possibility is that Joseph Smith Jr. was a complete fraud, the consummate con artist. This has been proposed and argued convincingly over the years. Scammers and charlatans have long used religion as a convenient, tax-exempt method for collecting donations from believing followers. There's little accountability and ample opportunity for diversion of funds. It's an excellent, respected vehicle for fraud.

Joseph was described as a lazy, directionless young man who relied on freelance digging in the ground for money and treasure as his occupation. Then he suddenly had a family to support and needed actual income. His record contains an early criminal charge for fraud.

The early 1800s in Joseph's geographic area was a time of religious fervor, itinerant preachers, tent-show revivals, and faith healings. Joseph may have seen such forms of money making as a more lucrative angle, and certainly less demanding than digging with a shovel for nonexistent treasure. When he met the affluent and religiously impressionable Martin Harris, he may have spotted his golden opportunity and reeled him in.

So, I give a definite maybe to this second possibility: Joseph Smith, a career criminal who creates his own flock and fleeces them.

But for me, as a medical doctor, I feel there is something deeper going on with Joseph. He may certainly have jumped at the chance to separate Martin Harris and others from their money, but the tone and words of the Book of Mormon struck me as indicative of a particular mental illness. Today that illness is known as bipolar disorder. For much of the twentieth century, it was known as manic depression. But back in the early 1800s, it didn't even have a name yet. This represents the third possibility.

I know it's hard to definitively diagnose somebody removed by space and time, but I developed strong suspicions early on in my reading of the Book of Mormon. The wordy, inflated, almost babbling speeches first caught my attention. As I trudged through the text, it began to dawn on me that I was witnessing a manic episode actually being recorded by a transcriptionist scribe. Toward the end of the book, the mania begins to subside. The previously detailed histories start to become abbreviated and even more repetitive. It's as if the author, Joseph Smith Jr, is running out of energy and ideas, and his manic phase is ending.

As far back as Ancient Rome and Greece, physicians described patients who exhibited severe mood swings—from periods of elation, with excessive energy and creativity, to sorrow, with markedly limited function. These up (manic) or down (depressive) phases are not day-to-day shifts. They each last for weeks or months at a time. Since Joseph's book dictation lasted a few months, this fits the time frame of a manic episode.

The disease didn't receive a name in the West until 1854, when French doctors Baillarger and Falret called it dual-form insanity, or circular insanity. In the early 1900s, German psychiatrist Emil Kraepelin gave it the name manic-depressive psychosis. He described periods of mania alternating with depressive phases, and also symptom-free intervals with normal functioning. The name was changed to bipolar disorder in the 1980s.

Bipolar disorder is a serious mental illness. The symptoms of a manic episode fit well with Joseph Smith's behavior. Patients exhibit frantic energy, fast speech, rambling and racing thoughts, and flights of ideas, and they take on huge creative projects. This matches Joseph's frenetic dictation of the lengthy Book of Mormon in near record time, with little sleep, and employing his magical accessories. You've got to admit—Joseph's book is creative.

Delusions and hallucinations, both auditory and visual, can also be experienced during mania. Joseph experienced visions of God, angels, and Moroni and regularly spoke with them. Hallucinations in mental illness are very commonly of a religious nature.

Manic patients often have grandiose, pompous, and exalted views of themselves, such as being a prophet, savior, deity, or messianic religious leader. That fits too. Joseph's projects certainly qualify as grandiose: saving mankind, establishing a New Zion, appointing himself general of his army, and even running for president of the United States.

The high energy of a manic phase also includes impulsivity and hypersexuality. These may explain Joseph's taking the wives and daughters of other Mormons for himself and dreaming up the doctrine of polygamy, even though it contradicted his teachings in the Book of Mormon. Impulsive decisions can also be seen in his constant moving of early Mormon settlements, corrupt banking, and shifty land deals.

Irritability, rage, and abrasiveness are also symptoms of the illness and are demonstrated by Joseph's reaction when Martin Harris "lost" the initial manuscript, his frequent disputes, and his "casting out" and excommunicating fellow Mormons from the Church.

Bipolar disorder typically first presents itself when someone is in their teens or twenties. This is exactly when Joseph experienced his hallucinations and dictated the Book of Mormon.

It also tends to occur in families, but is not necessarily passed to each child or generation. Recall that Joseph's grandfather also saw religious visions. There are reports that one of Joseph's sons became insane and was placed in a mental institution. This was the only treatment for manic-depressive illness at the time. Other reports claim that Joseph's later descendants also suffered from mental disorders and committed suicide. Bipolar patients have a significant risk of suicide.

Joseph Smith Jr. also experienced periods of depression. These aren't as well recorded since they don't have the glamour and excitement of manic phases. He was described as someone who was often lonely, withdrawn, and overwhelmed by events.

Bipolar disorder is frequently seen in actors, actresses, artists, writers, and creative types who sometimes achieve success and notoriety. Their capacity to produce large amounts of work and depict alternate interpretations of life contributes to their fame and also to their angst, depression, substance abuse, and higher suicide rates. The list of creative types with bipolar disorder can also include cult leaders and religious founders. It's easy to imagine Church of Scientology founder and prolific science fiction writer L. Ron Hubbard fitting the bill. Maybe even Jesus himself, or various saints, suffered from the illness, although we don't have enough reliable history to go on.

No treatment for this problem existed in Joseph Smith Jr.'s time. Since the advent of lithium medication in the 1970s, bipolar disorder is now successfully managed, but not cured.

Schizophrenia is another serious psychiatric disorder where patients hear voices, see visions, and harbor fantastic delusions. However, people with schizophrenia do not achieve social integration and popular success like those with bipolar disorder often do. Instead, people with schizophrenia are more likely to be withdrawn hermits, not charismatic leaders (think John the Baptist).

We'll never have conclusive proof of Joseph Smith Jr.'s mental condition, but to me it appears likely that he had bipolar disorder. Before I read the Book of Mormon, I suspected outright fraud was his primary motivation for creating the religion. Now that I have read it, I see him primarily as someone who had bipolar disorder, who also happened to have the amoral capacity to take advantage of others. After all, though those with untreated bipolar disorder typically have trouble with impulse control, the disorder says nothing about a person's moral compass.

I find it hard to imagine that a simple con artist would go through the trouble or even be capable of producing such a wild and elaborate religious history. Wouldn't it be much easier to just interpret and preach existing religious dogma, maybe with some minor twists, and start collecting contributions immediately, like a modern-day TV preacher? Coming up with such a litany of fictional names, events, places, and bombastic exhortations—all for the con—seems like a lot of extra work.

For me, it's much easier to imagine someone with bipolar disorder rapidly spewing an elaborate, nonsensical takeoff on religion during a manic episode than a simple con artist without such a condition. Merging his stories with the world of the early 1800s that he knew, he incorporated ideas, facts, and tropes familiar to him—whether taking from Old and New Testament verses, fiery preacher rants, racist attitudes, and basic military tactics, or American ideals of liberty, freedom, manifest destiny, democracy, and even antimonarchy rhetoric. This world also greatly informed what the Book of Mormon has to say about black and native peoples, whether directly or indirectly. These concepts form the basis of many of his rambling, flowery, borderline blathering passages, and his underlying beliefs serve as a foundation and springboard for his delusions and manic flights of ideas. Even after years of editing by the Church of Jesus Christ of Latter-day Saints, something to which they admit, the Book of Mormon is still sufficiently disjointed and delusional to qualify as mania.

Conclusion

Now that you have an idea of what is actually in the Book of Mormon, and how it originated, you can formulate your own opinion on this uniquely American religion that still dominates the lives of many contemporary believers. You can also use this newfound knowledge to gain insight about the worldview of its adherents, especially as they play an increasing role in American government and politics, and perhaps even to have an informed discussion with those Mormon missionaries who might knock on your door. If nothing else, you'll be better able to evaluate their claim recently popularized by the opening song in the Broadway play *The Book of Mormon*: "Hello! This book will change your life …"

About the Author

C. B. Brooks, M.D., is an author, physician, scuba dive master, volunteer firefighter, comedian, golfer, former policeman, and current parent. His goal is to bring clear and rational thinking to young and old alike, to cut through fake complexity, and to keep everyone laughing. He is the author of *Trust Your Radar*, *Trust Your Radar Slackers' Edition*, and *The Nonbeliever's Guide to Bible Stories*. He lives in New York City.